Being
Intentional

Making Work and Play
One and the Same

R. John Young

Design and Page Production by SPARK Publications
www.SPARKpublications.com

Published by Keane Publishing, Inc
www.keanepublishing.com

Printing History
First Edition, June 2014

Young, Ph.D., R. John
        Being Intentional, Making Work and Play One and the Same

ISBN 978-0-9854070-6-3
Library of Congress Control Number: 2014932811

Dedication

To my wife, Mary Pat, and our children, Moira and Seán

Endorsements

"I had the immense pleasure of observing Dr. Young's work with leaders of emerging democracies from across North Africa. Sponsored by the Bureau of International Information Programs, part of the United States Department of State, he helped them develop strategies to improve trust within their communities, develop the personal resiliency to cope with the stress and change the region is experiencing, and provide a 'Third Circle' for the organizations they lead. This book is a great addition to his toolkit."

—Riad Berdayi, Middle East Partnership Initiative Administrator,
United States Embassy, Rabat, Morocco

"Dr. Young not only guided and facilitated our organizational transition, he transformed our appreciation for what was possible, helped us confront both our strengths and some difficult realities, and brought us to a new level of trust and most importantly a collaborative, results-focused and responsive organization. His book provides valuable insights and wisdom directly relevant to elected officials regardless of the scale and scope of their communities."

—Don Borut, Former Executive Director,
National League of Cities, Washington, DC

"It is my belief that our students graduate with the foundational capacity to master each of the relationships that Dr. Young has identified in this unique book. He redesigns what it means to be a truly educated person."

—Dr. Glyn Cowlishaw, Head,
Providence Day School, Charlotte, NC

"It has been our pleasure to have Dr. Young work with our high potential and developing leaders. This book captures what it means to be a complete leader and a responsible citizen."

—Allen Gant, Chairman,
Glen Raven, Inc., Burlington, NC

"Skeptical by nature, I usually do not find leadership seminars particularly interesting. However, Dr. Young's seminar at Ballynahinch Castle was both invigorating and challenging. The location is stunning and the format personal—all of which helps add to the experience. For anyone trying to formulate a strategy in his or her head or work through a challenge this book and his seminar are essentials."

—Paschal McCarthy, Managing Director,
GE Healthcare, Bio-Sciences, Cork, Ireland

"This book truly helps the otherwise stressed out executive learn how to make work and play one and the same. It is a must read if you want to feel happy and fulfilled."

—Lance Mitchell, President and CEO,
Reynolds Consumer Products, Chicago, IL

"For over 25 years we have depended upon Dr. Young's expertise when confronted with the most challenging human capital issues. His guidance has helped us navigate the complex organizational/cultural changes necessary to complement our strategic direction, coach our leaders, and help troubled employees and their families. His approach addresses issues at the most fundamental levels related to organizational and individual health. This book illustrates the interdependence of our multiple roles as a professional, a partner, a parent, a leader, and a citizen and poses the challenge: "Imagine how and what you want to be.""

—Nick Rodono, Senior Vice President, Human Resources,
National Gypsum Company, Charlotte, NC

"For many years Dr. Young has helped us nurture the best trained, most effective leaders in the nonprofit world. He works with every new cohort entering our Executive Development Program using the principles outlined in this book. Our leaders consistently note that he uniquely integrates the personal and professional challenges they confront."

—Lane Schonour, Executive Development Program Director,
Goodwill Industries International, Rockville, MD

KEANE PUBLISHING, INC.

Also by R. John Young

The Five Essential Leadership Questions:
Living With Passion, Leading Through Trust

www.keanepublishing.com

Contents

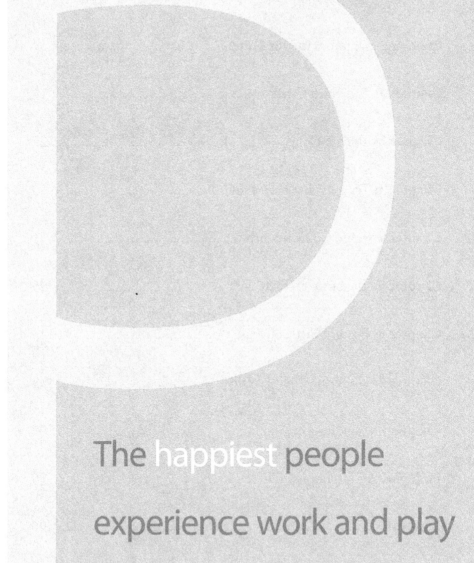

The happiest people
experience work and play
as one and the same.

Happiness in Our Time

In this book I identify what I believe are the six most important relationships that are subtly intertwined but, when optimal, open the *doors* to true success and happiness.

First among them is the relationship with one's profession; second is the intimacy and support from a life partner; third is the satisfaction from raising emotionally healthy children; fourth is the respect from being a trusted and effective leader; fifth is the security of having loyal clients and customers; sixth is the relevance of contributing and belonging to a nurturing community.

If you hope to survive a successful career and enjoy happiness in your time, you will be wise to intentionally pursue and own a deeper understanding of the determinants of true success, happiness, and profitability rather than settle for a mediocre existence.

I work with too many executives who seem to have no appreciation for the human factors that shape the success of their enterprises, both domestic and professional, until they have lost everything—their professional statuses, their marriages, their children, the trust of their employees and shareholders, the loyalty of their customers, and meaningful roles in their communities.

They seem to be blind as to how their choices today may align to compromise their future judgments or critical decision making.

Are they scared to open the Pandora's Box or the *doors* that might change their lives forever? Or do they assume that these challenges are so out of their control that they learn to be helpless and tightly lock down the *door* that might otherwise liberate their passions?

Consider this: The relationships we have with our professions are somewhat selfish and all about us. The relationships we have with our life partners are a little more altruistic. The relationships we have with our children are even more altruistic. We are paid to be leaders and to serve our customers. But the relationships we have with our communities are the most altruistic of all.

As a result of the range and radius of my work within organizations and communities, I see so clearly that a distraction in any one of these relationships will be reflected within each of the others and will eventually compromise an executive's ability to adapt.

> We adapt and change either by shock, evolution, or anticipation.

When we fail to adapt, figuratively speaking, we die.

The ability to adapt and solve problems is the primary determinant of personal and organizational health. We adapt and change either by shock, evolution, or anticipation. Shock comes with natural disasters or untimely loss. Evolution is the inevitable consequence of the aging process. Anticipation is taking a positive and proactive orientation toward destiny, almost to the point of being change-welcoming; anticipation is being intentional.

You cannot remake the bed while you are still in it! Sometimes you will have to detach yourself from a situation and remake your world. I encourage my clients to start by taking a scientific approach to change. I remind them that the first step in science is observation. And, as with learning the performance attributes of any sport, the first challenge is to relax.

Each of the relationships I have identified in this book is at risk from the ubiquitous loss of trust, unrelenting stress, and the weak, platitude-ridden leadership that results from the absence of what I call a "Third Circle©."

To that end, I have incorporated all of the psychosocial theories and practices relating to change into my **Third Circle** concept (chapter 1). Because of its simplicity, it is extremely powerful in helping my clients diagnose past failures, define their futures intentionally, align everything with those definitions, leverage their existing strengths, ruthlessly confront the saboteurs, and motivate themselves to reach their "Third Circles."

Initially, I conceived the "Third Circle" as a way of helping leaders quickly see their challenges and find their leadership voices. As I would unfold it, either with a twig in the African soil or on a paper napkin in a restaurant, I noticed that my clients' eyes would glaze over. Soon I came to realize that they were privately applying its precepts to their personal lives. They were asking themselves whether they had "Third Circles" for their own leadership, their marriages, or their parenting. They began to listen differently to their political leaders. They observed the condition of their communities more critically. I also noticed that the absence of a "Third Circle" foretold a certain kind of emptiness, or something missing in their lives. God forbid that they are asked to follow someone who did not have a "Third Circle!"

> Too often they mechanically recite vision and mission statements that have been reduced to PowerPoint platitudes.

Sadly, much of the management training delivered during the last 40 years may have worked against managers' ability to articulate a "Third Circle." Too often they mechanically recite vision and mission statements that have been reduced to PowerPoint platitudes. Too many of the executives I work with cannot, without any props, articulate the stated vision, mission, or values of their businesses. The late Steve Jobs, co-founder, chairman, and chief executive officer of Apple, Inc., recalled, "People would confront a problem by creating a presentation. I wanted them to engage, to hash things out at the table, rather than show a bunch of slides. People who know what they're talking about don't need PowerPoint."

The **Third Circle** concept, in contrast, requires the leader to understand and explain why the current situation is untenable, articulate passionately where she is committed to taking the enterprise, be believable about the effectiveness of the strategies she is proposing in order to attain that destiny, and provide a sense of safeness that she can make it a reality.

In the following chapters, I will introduce you to my **Third Circle** concept and how it can help you intentionally select a career to which you can passionately commit; choose a life partner with whom you can enjoy enduring intimacy; raise emotionally healthy children; develop the competencies required to become a trusted and effective leader; secure the trust and loyalty of your clients and customers; and be part of creating a nurturing community.

In no way do I undervalue the importance of your financial acumen and fiduciary responsibility in the management of your family or your business. For the purposes of this book, they are assumed. However, this book exposes the unspoken criteria that business owners, corporate directors, or citizens intuitively know and use to evaluate and select those to whom they entrust the leadership of their organizations or communities.

These are the criteria that determine whether an executive retires with the sense of pride and accomplishment that derives from having taken his organization to its potential "Third Circle" or with the sense of sadness that comes from having lost the trust and effectiveness within the critical relationships that underpin *true* success, happiness, and profitability.

When you intentionally pursue and demonstrate mastery in each of the relationships identified in this book, and know how to leverage their collective power, work and play will be one and the same, and you will have identified how to be happy in your time.

All great leaders, as well as those who achieve their personal dreams, feel entitled to their "Third Circles" and are intentional about achieving them.

CHAPTER 1

The Third Circle

It doesn't work to leap a twenty-foot chasm in two ten-foot jumps. *—American proverb*

When we study those who truly succeed in life and for whom work and play are one and the same, we find that they secure an accurate diagnosis of their current statuses. This enables them to unleash the creativity and innovation to define their futures boldly; align everything logically and strategically with those definitions; leverage all of the talent at their disposal; summon up the courage to confront the saboteurs; and commit the personal energy to make the leap across the chasm to, what I call, the "Third Circle."

Abraham Lincoln observed, "People are just as happy as they make up their minds to be." Are you happy? Are you pursuing your ideal career? Is your family a source of comfort and empowerment? Are you clear about where you are leading your business? Do you embrace change, or are you its victim? Are you *being intentional?*

After years of studying change theories and helping my clients implement change strategies, I realized that I could significantly simplify how we talk about change. I am convinced that organizational development professionals over-complicate change. To be sure, anthropology, psychology, and the other social sciences have contributed enormously to our scientific understanding of human motivation and behavior. However, to me, change is as simple as one-two-three! And change will never stick if you do not have a "Third Circle" or if you cannot intentionally open the *doors* to reach it.

When introducing my clients to the **Third Circle** concept, regardless of their intellectual or financial sophistication, I like to break their preoccupation by drawing three circles horizontally in a row either on a white board, a paper tablet, a napkin, or as I did in Africa, in the dusty soil. In the "First Circle" I write the words *Pain* and *Desire*.

I then draw an arrow moving to the right, toward the "Third Circle." I abruptly stop it, however, at a vertical line drawn down through the middle of the "Second Circle," which I call *The Wall*.

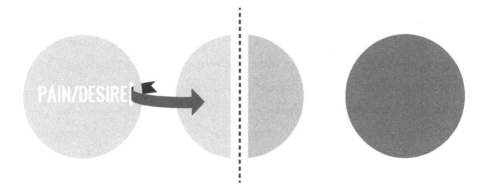

I then draw repetitive loops between the "First Circle" and *The Wall* symbolizing the addictive and helpless trap into which so many of us succumb when attempting to extricate ourselves from an unhappy or unprofitable career, relationship, business, or community.

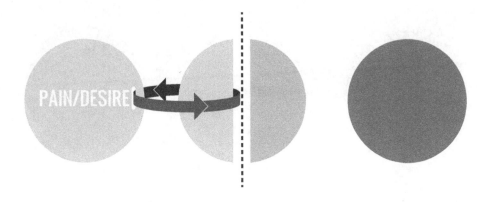

I then write the word *Ideal* within the "Third Circle," purposefully avoiding, for reasons which will later become clear, the use of the word *Vision*.

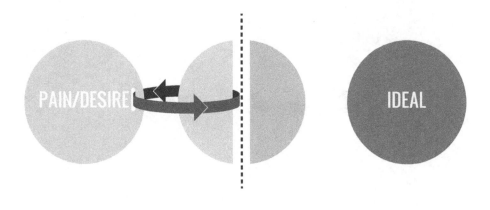

Within the "Second Circle," but to the right of *The Wall*, I iterate, bullet-like, the tasks that must be accomplished to generate the momentum required to traverse the chasm between the "Second Circle" and the "Third Circle."

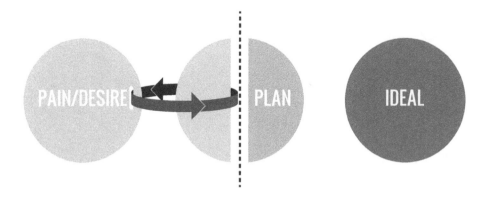

I dramatize that traversing with a bold arrow and remind my clients that they cannot leap a twenty-foot chasm in two ten-foot jumps!

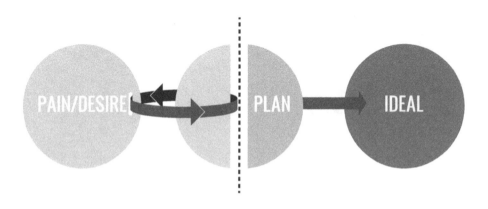

Above that chasm I write the word *Leverage* to indicate the importance of harnessing all the creativity, diversity, and talent at our disposal.

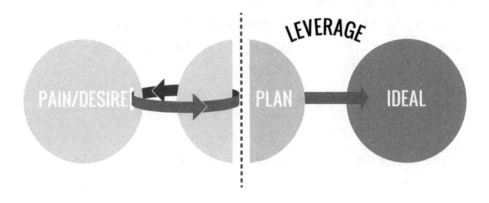

Below the chasm I write the word *Saboteurs* to accentuate the importance of those forces within or around us that, if not confronted, will undoubtedly compromise our abilities to reach our "Third Circles."

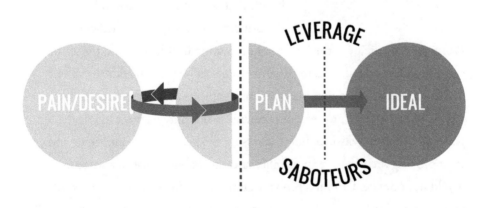

All great leaders, as well as those who achieve their personal dreams, feel entitled to their "Third Circles" and are intentional about achieving them. Bono, the primary vocalist and lyricist of the Dublin-based rock band U2, reflecting on the passing of Nelson Mandela, observed: "He was able to see a future even before it exists."

Can you see the military general describing for his staff the campaign he is about to launch? Can you hear the authority and succinctness with which he speaks? Is his "Third Circle" non-negotiable?

Interestingly, for all the talk these days about leadership, it is my observation that most chief executives would love to have their senior executives collaborate instead of feuding, undermining, or sabotaging each other.

As I mentioned earlier, I first encounter my clients, whether individuals, organizations, or communities, when they are in their "First Circles." Their respective "First Circles" are their current situations, often characterized by either pain or desire. As a consultant, this phase is like being in the boxing ring with a kangaroo! I never know from where the left upper cut may come! Whether they ask for my support or not, to my clients, I represent change.

This audit is quite sophisticated since it uses an approach to organizational health that is strongly influenced by the principles of prospective medicine. Prospective medicine is the science of estimating health risks and the art of communicating those risks to patients/clients to help them address current health concerns and to make choices that improve their long-term health.

The technology of prospective medicine is not only relevant to improving personal health but also applies to assessing the health of organizations and to improving their long-term viability and profitability. Just as a surgeon would not operate without a proper examination, an accurate diagnosis of organizational risks must be made in order for appropriate and effective interventions to be prescribed and executed. Here too we need to abandon the heroic approaches to organizational health and base our strategies on much sounder intelligence.

An organizational diagnosis includes understanding the genetics of the business—for example, governance, structure, and legacy issues, such as those associated with mergers or acquisitions. Culture includes such things as values systems, symbolic structures, and traditions. The organizational equivalent of lifestyle includes how people lead, collaborate, and follow. Interestingly, for all the talk these days about leadership, it is my observation that most chief executives would love to have their senior executives collaborate instead of feuding, undermining, or sabotaging each other.

Have you learned not *to achieve your dreams?*

What is your family history, or how did your organization evolve? How is your business governed? How is it structured and organized? What cultural legacy issues did you inherit by virtue of the acquisitions you may have made?

How well-developed are your personal and your company's values? Are they being lived? How are they being promulgated? What holds your family or your company together? What do others see when they encounter you; what image do they take away?

Where does your authority come from? How often is it challenged? Whether at home or at work, how are solutions derived? Do you know when to defer to others who may have a better solution?

The "Second Circle" contains *The Wall* that people and organizations so often hit as they try to get to their idealized "Third Circle." Too often they keep repeating the same mistakes, circling back and forth between the first and second circles. *The wall* may be like a pane of glass in that people think they see their "Third Circle" but cannot pass through the invisible wall. Alternately, it may be like a brick wall in that they cannot see over or beyond it, and they remain oblivious as to the possibilities that lie beyond the wall.

If you are honest with yourself, are you repeatedly trying to change something? Have you given up on losing weight, stopping smoking, finding the right job, finding the right partner? Have you learned *not* to achieve your dreams?

As you can see, these obstacles are on all fronts of our lives. They impact nations, communities, corporations, and homes. Witness the challenge that the European Union is experiencing as some of its member states are forced to confront the realities of their financial conditions. In the absence of "Third Circle" leadership and a "Third Circle" culture they run the risk of oscillating between their first and second circles with all the uncertainty and fears.

> Lack of creativity and innovation are the greatest culprits when countries go to war, communities decay, businesses fail, couples split, and soccer teams lose.

The nationalistic example can be extended beyond financial crises to examples of cultural tragedy. For example, is there "Third Circle" leadership in the Middle East or a "Third Circle" for the region?

What countries do you perceive are pursuing their "Third Circles?" Do you think that China has a "Third Circle?" Does South Korea? Does North Korea?

While the 2012 Summer Olympic Games in London had within them many examples of individual "Third Circle" athletic pursuits, London's embrace of the Olympic Games exemplified a community and a nation's commitment to a "Third Circle." I watched the games with personal interest. My family moved to London from Ireland in 1951, not long after the end of the Second World War.

To this day I can recall the bombed out craters; the frequent discovery of unexploded bombs; the almost daily requests from people wanting to rent a room; the disquieting sight of people collapsing from either untreated epilepsy or what we now call post-traumatic stress; and the air raid shelter in the back garden. I can still remember the smell and the suffocating feeling from donning the gas masks that my sisters and I found in the attic.

Those were very minimalist times. Everything was scarce. We bought food with rationing coupons. A bicycle was a luxury. I can still see the swarm of black bicycles ridden by gray-clad men and women racing to their work at the EMI factory, famous for the iconic His Master's Voice record label.

I left London on a dark and dreary January day in 1971 to pursue graduate studies at Purdue University in Indiana. Over the years, I returned regularly to be with family. So, the transformation that London achieved through the guidance of the "Third Circle" it created upon the award of hosting the Summer Olympics was striking. To Great Britain, staging the Olympic Games was more than a set of athletic contests. It was an opportunity to reinvent itself after many difficult decades characterized by economic and social challenges. It was an opportunity to regain the social cohesion it enjoyed before the Second World War. During the Olympics, London was dazzling. Its residents were the happiest I can remember.

> As poetry is to literature; so the "Third Circle" is to change.

The "Third Circle" is the ideal state to which we aspire—our "brands." Like the London Olympics, nothing can happen until it is imagined. Lack of creativity and innovation are the greatest culprits when countries go to war, communities decay, businesses fail, couples split, and soccer teams lose. However, effective idealism starts with a brutally realistic assessment of the "First Circle." Often that is not possible until we have failed and learned from those failures.

As I alluded to earlier, the "Third Circle" is much more than the recitation of a vision statement. In truth, most employees have switched off to the often indistinguishable sentences that constitute vision statements. Moreover, the stress and lack of trust they experience these days leaves them feeling unsafe and reluctant to engage. In contrast, the person with a "Third Circle" transforms that vision into a total presence and authenticity with the capacity to articulate its promise, create safeness, engender hope, and command the attention of those they lead.

As poetry is to literature, so the "Third Circle" is to change. Because of its simplicity and animation, the Third Circle concept has proven to be extremely powerful in helping my clients see the need for change, acknowledge past failures, imagine the ideal state, and then make it happen. To make it happen, however, they must have the desire and the courage to open *six doors* and master the challenges that lie beyond them. They must be intentional.

Reflective Questions

- What is your "Third Circle?"
  Are you being intentional about pursuing it?

- What talents do you possess that are not being recognized
  or leveraged?

- What are the saboteurs that can prevent your achieving
  the "Third Circle?"

To be sure, the *doors*

we open and close

each day decide our

lives. They can protect

us or hold us prisoner.

CHAPTER 2

The Six Doors

The doors we open and close each day decide the lives we live. *—Flora Whittemore*

A former participant in our seminar "Trusted and Effective Leadership: Reclaiming the Creativity to Lead Change" that we conduct at Ballynahinch Castle in the west of Ireland, called me recently to schedule a lunch meeting. Jim is a local professional whom I have known for several years and have worked with periodically. I invited him to the seminar because he was extremely frustrated with the course of his career. His "First Circle" pain was palpable. He could fantasize about his "Third Circle" but felt immobilized when it came to pursuing it. He was stuck, scared, and very unhappy. Work and play were certainly not one and the same. Moreover, he was extremely introverted, rule-bound, and cautious.

As the seminar unfolded, it became clear that he was frustrated with himself and with his company. It showed itself in the way in which he went back and forth between blaming himself and blaming his company. He was waiting for the company to change to allow him to express his potential. When Jim realized that his company was not going to change, he became very frustrated and angry.

By way of background, the venue for our seminar is in one of the most serene, stress-free, and creative environments in the world. It is an escape from all distractions and stress. The recreational periods are as important as the relaxed, yet intellectually challenging, conversations and discussions in front of the log fire. The formal component of the seminar is held between 8:00 am and 2:00 pm.

After lunch we explore the region around the castle known as Connemara in County Galway. Connemara is one of the last unspoiled parts of Europe. We explore its mountains and lakes and observe example after example of how its inhabitants have, across generations, survived and flourished against all odds. This creativity and resiliency is a wonderful metaphor for the lessons of the seminar.

> Many senior executives are held prisoner by those around them, the structure they have created, or by their rearing. It is very lonely at the top.

The third dimension to the seminar is the evening activities. After a magnificent dinner in the castle's dining room, we convene, along with other guests, in the castle bar. Traditionally, my co-facilitator, Fintan Muldoon, who is also an excellent musician, plays the piano and gently and unthreateningly uncovers the diversity of talent in the room. Needless to say, Jim was noticeably uncomfortable, stood back, and avoided social interaction both in the afternoon and evening's activities.

By the last afternoon, Jim recognized that his "Third Circle" involved a vision of how he would like to see his future. Fintan suggested, again in his unthreatening manner, that he open the metaphorical *door*. This served three purposes: first, it validated for Jim that he was in charge of creating the "Third Circle" for himself; second, it helped him see that getting angry at the company was counter-productive; and third, it reminded him that he was in control of the situation and, therefore, was the one who had to take the step to actually open the *door*. As the German proverb exalts us, "The greatest step is out the *door*."

The seminar helped Jim crystallize his "Third Circle." It gave him a clear *intellectual* understanding of his dilemma. It also allowed him to understand that he was in control of achieving it. Finally, it started the process of developing the *emotional* courage to actually open the *door*.

During our lunch, Jim shared with me that, as a result of participating in the seminar, he was able to summon up the courage to "turn the knob" and reclaim a new life. It was the turning point in reinventing his career and regaining his happiness. To be sure, the *doors* we open and close each day decide our lives. They can protect us or hold us prisoner. Many senior executives are held prisoner by those around them, the structure they have created, or by their rearing. It is very lonely at the top.

Jim's experience is far from uncommon. In truth, it is but one example of the fears that manifest themselves early in the journey to our "Third Circles." The scholars, consultants, and clinicians in my company use the **Third Circle** concept every day to help their clients understand their "First Circles," clearly see their "Third Circles," and proceed through the sequential *doors* to its realization.

There are six *doors* through which a person, a couple, a family, a business, a community, or even a nation moves on its way to the "Third Circle."

Door One is the *door* we must open if we are to understand and diagnose our "First Circles." The "First Circle" is typically characterized by pain or desire, the most basic of human motivations. Can you describe the futility of past attempts to change and the resulting denial, the learned helplessness, or the external locus of control? Remember that, as within the human body, pain is referred, meaning that it may be felt some distance from where it is originating. Heart attacks, for example, may be felt down the arm or up the neck.

This may be the most important *door* since diagnosis determines strategy. So many attempts to change are initiated by well-intentioned motivational or inspirational efforts that quickly fizzle, much like a New Year's resolution.

Door 1

A diagnosis that fleshes out the genetic, cultural, lifestyle, and access to care impediments to change is the differentiator between a scientific approach to change and naïve cheer-leading.

When we hit *The Wall*, our normal coping mechanisms are no longer effective. We are often mistakenly convinced that we can reach the "Third Circle" on our own.

Recently, a clinician in my company counseled a young woman who had come to use the services of our employee assistance program. When the counselor shared with her the **Third Circle** concept as a way of explaining her experiences to date, she exclaimed that, after many years of personal experience with addiction, the **Third Circle** concept offered, in her opinion, the most powerful construct to gain an addict's attention and commitment.

Door Two is the *door* in the wall that we must locate and either pry open or blast through if we are to claim our "Third Circle." "Every wall is a door," wrote Ralph Waldo Emerson. As I mentioned earlier, the wall may be transparent, or it may be solid. Regardless, it has to be either scaled or penetrated.

"Follow your bliss," wrote Joseph Campbell, the Irish American mythologist and scholar of comparative religion, "and the universe will open doors for you where there were only walls." A small key opens big doors. Fintan gave Jim the key to the big *door* that held him prisoner.

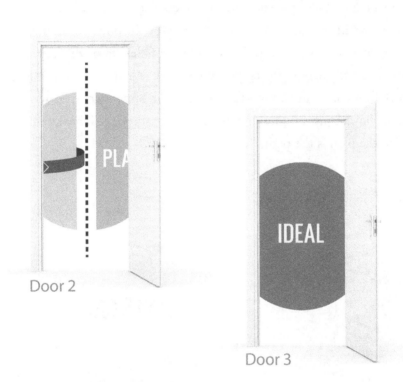

Door 2

Door 3

Door Three is the *door* that unlocks our imaginations and where we can see the ideal state, the "Third Circle," clearly in our minds' eyes. Happy and intentional people are able to describe their "Third Circles" and attract others to also believe in that ideal. In the words of Henry Miller—considered a literary innovator in whose works actual and imagined experiences became indistinguishable from each other—"The real leader has no need to lead—he is content to point the way." They can do this with conviction and without the typical platitudes to which their life partners, children, or employees have, like children to antibiotics, developed a tolerance! In some instances we have to implant a dream.

Door Four is the *door* that we must open to reveal a clear description of what it will take to get to the "Third Circle." Need teaches a plan. Here the plan includes the strategies and tactics that, if properly executed, and in the right sequence, will provide the power to traverse the chasm between the "Second" and "Third Circles" into which so many well-intentioned change efforts typically plunge. Again, you cannot leap a twenty-foot chasm in two ten-foot jumps! Too often executives start with the plan, or just build on previous plans, without a "Third Circle" to which the plan is the path.

Door 4

Door 5

Door Five, when opened, reveals all the creativity and innovation that is waiting to be unleashed. It permits talent identification, management, and leverage. Do you know what kind of work gives you joy and satisfaction?

Do you know what you need from your life partner? Do you acknowledge the uniqueness of your children's temperaments and aspirations? Do you know your employees and your customers? Do you respect your fellow citizens? Do you listen? Do you communicate or tell?

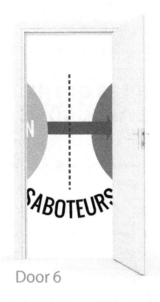

Door 6

Door Six exposes the potential saboteurs of the plan's implementation. Opening it permits the declaration of what is, for you, non-negotiable, and your willingness to act on the obvious. "All of the great leaders have had one characteristic in common," noted John Kenneth Galbraith, arguably the best known economist in the world during his lifetime having served in the administrations of presidents Roosevelt, Truman, Kennedy and Johnson. "It was the willingness to confront unequivocally the major anxiety of their people in their time. This, and not much else, is the essence of leadership."

When you have passed through all six *doors* you will have attained a new self or new organization with optimal passion and vitality. It is finding that career where work and play is one and the same thing. It is enjoying a marriage of mutual admiration. It is watching a child pursue his or her dream with focus and commitment. It is the confidence you feel as a leader when you know exactly where to take the business. It is the respect you feel when your customers are loyal to your products and services. It is the tranquility and safeness that pervades your community.

Too often people fall into the trap of trying to work on each *door* at the same time. Partition the problem. What you learn about your "First Circle" will influence how you tackle the second *door*, and so on.

THERE ARE EXAMPLES OF THE THIRD CIRCLE ALL AROUND US

I regularly challenge my clients to just look around at all the living examples of people either opening or closing *doors* as they pursue, or fail to pursue, their "Third Circles." For example, I was struck by a recent documentary about Al Buehler, the legendary Duke University track coach and educator. Amy Unell's documentary is based on her book *Starting at the Finish Line: Coach Al Buehler's Timeless Wisdom*[1]. The title is a perfect illustration of the **Third Circle** concept.

Al Buehler arrived at Duke University in 1955, following a tour as an Air Force captain during the Korean War. He was a track standout at Maryland and also head coach of the cross country team. In 1964 he was promoted from assistant to head track and field coach. During his career, he coached five Olympians at Duke and served as team manager for the United States Summer Olympic teams in 1972, 1984, and 1988. At age 70, he served as head manager for the United States team in the 2001 World Indoor Track Championships in Portugal.

Coach Buehler's life and career epitomize someone with a "Third Circle." Moreover, the course he taught on the history and issues in American sport examined the character, passion, and commitment required to excel in sports. It was he who, in 1968, drove John Carlos and Tommie Smith to the Mexico City airport when they were removed from the United States Olympic team for their defiant salute on the medal-stand. At the Munich Olympic Games in 1972 he was just a hundred yards from the massacre.

Buehler's character and the way he lived spoke more than those accomplishments. For example, Dr. Leroy Walker, North Carolina Central's track coach, was his best friend. At the height of the racial tensions in the segregated South, Duke's track team practiced with Walker's all-black squad at Duke's track at a time when its campus and the bleachers above the track were segregated. He often quoted from Cicero's essay "On Friendship": "*Esse quam videri*—to be, rather than to seem (to be)."

Whether as a professional, a partner, a parent, a leader, a vendor, or a citizen, it is essential to imagine how and what you want to be. "What we really want to do is what we are really meant to do," wrote the artist Julia Cameron. "When we do what we are meant to do, money comes to us, doors open for us, we feel useful, and the work we do feels like play to us."

Each year my company deals with hundreds of applications of the **Third Circle** concept; but one encounter, in a manufacturing facility in Detroit, brought home to me the potency of the construct. This particular plant had experienced a union lockout eight years earlier and before my involvement with the facility. Employees hated coming to work and could not wait to leave after eight hours. There was an incredible amount of anger. Even younger employees who had been employed only a few months were protesting about the lockout years before their time.

When I drew the "Third Circle" in group meetings, I could see the blood drain out of the employees' faces. I would graphically describe the attempt toward the "Third Circle," hitting the invisible wall and then circling back to the "First Circle."

Failure characterized everything they attempted. They saw their lives, both personal and professional, pass before their eyes. They argued that all they needed was more money. I told them that I had no control over their compensation, but that I could impact their ability to see their "Third Circles," understand the *doors* they had to open to achieve it, and do what it would take to realize their dreams, whether within the plant or elsewhere. If they chose to stay, at least it would be voluntary. If they chose to leave, they were in charge of their own destinies.

That meeting, tense as it was, was the turning point in changing the hearts and minds of that workforce. The anger was abated. Employees and managers began listening to each other and, instead of confrontation, cooperation became the norm. The work of changing the culture finally began.

Routinely, we use the **Third Circle** concept to help our client organizations improve their effectiveness, productivity, and profitability. In contrast to a complicated "electrical wiring diagram" characterizing organizational development, the simplicity of the **Third Circle** concept is quickly understood and appreciated. Employees at all levels can share a language about change and accept accountability for their respective roles in the change process.

> Whether as a professional, a partner, a parent, a leader, a vendor, or a citizen, it is essential to imagine how and what you want to be.

When you *get* the **Third Circle** concept and identify the *doors* you must open, those who do not have a "Third Circle" become nakedly obvious to you. They stand out for their lack of focus, believability, and conviction. They do not have willing followers and, instead, resort to blaming others for their failures, known in clinical circles as "blaming the victim."

Recently I presented the **Third Circle** concept to the owner of a major textile company in the southern United States. After reflecting on what I had presented he asked, "How many people realize their 'Third Circles'?" The question was quite profound. Too often we look for proxy measures such as household income, educational level, or marital status to estimate that percentage. Individually these are poor predictors. In truth, the *grand* "Third Circle" reflects how well-integrated career, marriage, child-rearing, business leadership, and social responsibility are.

A few years ago, I began coaching the divisional president of a $3 billion public corporation in the United States. Eventually, this person ascended to the chief executive role for the whole corporation. A year later, I received a call from the chairman of the board concerned about the performance of the company and the leadership provided by its new chief executive. After careful analysis, it became clear that the chief executive had not declared a "Third Circle" for the business he now led. Arguably, such a declaration is the number one responsibility of the chief executive. Only he or she can provide it.

This particular company had enjoyed reasonable organic growth but, typically, had collected a variety of related businesses along with their genetic cultural material. The frugality of the previous chief executive, who stayed around during a transitional year, combined with his strong personality inhibited the boldness required of the new chief executive when he assumed the helm.

Fortunately, once all concerned *got* the **Third Circle** concept, they saw how inadequate the communication had become with the investor community, how the leadership team was not really a team, and how the workforce had no idea where the company was going. In fact, employees reported difficulty describing the business they worked for to their friends. The company had become a collection of brands. It was hard to discern the *soul* of the business. They had and were doing "stuff." The kind of "stuff" they had done for years disconnected from the rigor a plan to realize a "Third Circle" would demand. They were creating organizational noise instead of clarity.

When you *get* the Third Circle concept and identify the *doors* you must open, those who do not have a "Third Circle" become nakedly obvious to you.

As a coach and adviser to senior executives, I require my clients to clearly articulate their "Third Circles." This is what differentiates the espouser of platitudes about leadership from the person who can truly define the *soul* of his or her business, engender trust throughout, replace stress with hope, describe how his or her vision will be realized, leverage all the talent within, and confront the saboteurs.

This person is clear about what is non-negotiable. He does not label his employees as being resistant to change. Instead he can stand up and, without any props, sell his "Third Circle" to those who must buy-in for the success of the enterprise. "Avoid clichés like the plague," William Safire, the late syndicated columnist, etymologist, and presidential speechwriter, chastised us.

Observe how few executives are capable of standing in front of investors, directors, colleagues, or employees and, without their dependency on modern-day props, inspire those witnesses with the clarity of their visions, their ownership of the factors of success, and their abilities to create safeness in an era of disbelief and distrust. In truth, the more they persist with their inadequacy, the larger the human capital debt they create for themselves—one from which they are unlikely to recover.

> This is what differentiates the espouser of platitudes about leadership from the person who can truly define the *soul* of his or her business, engender trust throughout, replace stress with hope, describe how his or her vision will be realized, leverage all the talent within, and confront the saboteurs.

In the corporate world, human capital is the critical determinant of innovation, productivity, and organizational resiliency. As I have argued here and in my earlier book, the future belongs to those who understand the power of human capital and know how to harness it. But it is a grossly under-developed competency and one that has been largely over-bureaucratized or conversely left to those to whom it comes naturally.

If our businesses are to maintain their competitive edges, we must attract and develop the strongest human resources talent and empower them with both the science and the artistry for human capital development. Time is of the essence. We are paying the price for the fickleness of the last thirty years. Employees are rapidly disengaging. They do not know whom to trust. Moreover, they are vulnerable to the presentation of "Third Circles" that are less than wholesome or downright evil.

A "Third Circle" has integrity, proportionality, and beauty. If well-conceived with the *doors* identified, it will engender trust and believability within those expected to embrace it. It will not be too big or too small, and it will feel right. A "Third Circle" is a beautiful objective, so clearly manageable and so obviously the right thing to do.

If you do not have a "Third Circle," you will become part of someone else's! For example, recently a district attorney heard me talk and followed up with a request to meet for lunch. My presentation had stimulated some reflection in him about the performance of his department. As we discussed his challenges and frustrations, it became clear to him that the defendant's lawyers often had a more compelling "Third Circle" for a particular case than did the district attorney's lawyers. Instead of securing convictions in cases that seemed clear cut, his lawyers were not as motivated to secure a conviction or were out-maneuvered and allowed themselves to become part of the defendant's lawyers' "Third Circle."

> A "Third Circle" has integrity, proportionality and beauty.

Political contests are among the most poignant examples of "Third Circle" ownership—or not. Voters subconsciously listen for "Third Circles" from their candidates. Intuitively they can discern whether or not the candidate *gets* the "First Circle"; can articulate his or her "Third Circle"; knows how to open the *doors* to get there and, like President Ronald Reagan confronting President Mikhail Gorbachev over the Berlin wall, has the courage to call out the saboteurs. How we "experience" a political candidate is crucial to his or her success. But, like their corporate counterparts, too many candidates still resort to crude manipulation.

Regardless of your political affiliation, President Barack Obama's

> If you do not have a "Third Circle," you will become part of someone else's!

candidacy for the 2008 presidential campaign was a contemporary example of the use of the **Third Circle** concept in the political arena. At the outset of the campaign, he described the nation's "First Circle" and what he perceived were the negative consequences of the incumbent administration's policies.

He then forcefully described his "Third Circle" and the one he imagined for the country. He did this up until approximately four months before the election. He then returned the conversation to the second half of the "Second Circle" and began to provide some detail for how he thought the country could actually reach its "Third Circle," what it had to leverage, and the potential saboteurs that could derail that possibility. In essence, he was asserting that he could be a trusted and effective leader.

My work with community leaders continually reminds me that winning an election is quite different from governing. I will pick up this thought again in chapter 8.

Be warned: "We do not pass through the same door twice," wrote T. S. Eliot, "or return to the door through which we did not pass."

Reflective Questions

■ Which *door* is the hardest for you to open?

■ How do you respond to change?
Do you welcome it, pursue it, or fear it? Why?

■ Describe your *Wall*. What does it feel like to you?

No one cares more about your career than you do. So take charge of it. Be intentional.

CHAPTER 3

The First Big Decision

Choose a job you love, and you will never have to work a day in your life. *—Confucius*

Arguably, the two most important choices we make in life and that impact our happiness are the careers we pursue and the life partners to whom we commit and count on for support. The success or failure of either is so dependent upon the other. Sequentially, however, the embarkation upon a career usually precedes the commitment to our life partners. In truth, the latter is often predicated upon the former.

I recently worked with a well-educated young woman who was employed at a leading financial institution but, like Jim, our seminar participant, Deidre was experiencing a difficult time in her life and career. She presented as very put together and ambitious but reported that she had hit a *wall* and was unable to make progress in her professional life as well as in her interpersonal relationships outside of work.

Deidre's desire was to become an executive at the bank where she had worked for over ten years. She liked her work, and her performance reviews were above average. She was often given big projects, but even with their successful completion she could not open the *door* to the executive strata. She also reported struggles maintaining close personal relationships with other women.

When I drew the three circles model, Deidre put both the pain of rejection and the desire to be promoted in her "First Circle." Her "Third Circle" initially came easy. She claimed that it was to achieve executive status; but, upon closer examination, what also became a part of her "Third Circle" was to have more friends.

After processing that ideal state, she divulged that she often felt as though she was not good enough and that her friends got tired of being around her. Too often, she felt that she did more for her friends than they would ever do for her. When I asked her to consider what might be sabotaging her efforts to achieve her "Third Circles" she timidly stated that she worked in a male-dominated culture and had a succession of supervisors, none of whom were able to really get to know her.

> Career choices have their roots very early in life and are not always positive, for they can be fraught with biases and prejudices.

In her personal life, Deidre felt as though other women were mean. She had become distrustful of her friends' motives and generally felt that they were fair-weather friends. I challenged her to go deeper, and one of the things that we were able to identify as sabotaging her from achieving her "Third Circle" was her own attitude and her view of herself as the victim in situations.

With the exposure of these painful saboteurs, she was able to identify what she could leverage to feel more accepted, have deeper relationships, and succeed at work. She created a detailed plan to work on knowing herself and others more richly, demonstrating respect to herself and others, listening more openly, communicating more effectively, and building healthy relationships in all of the domains of her life.

Like Jim, Deidre was not as happy as she expected to be. The reasons were slightly different from Jim's, but I also invited her to "put the oxygen mask on herself first" as flight attendants remind us before take-off.

HOW DID YOU CHOOSE YOUR CAREER?

Career choices have their roots very early in life and are not always positive, for they can be fraught with biases and prejudices. As a grandparent, I have noted how early we discuss careers with children, often through stories or nursery rhymes. What role are they going to play in the community? Will they be the mayor, the policeman, the fireman, or whomever? Recall how early in our lives our parents or our aunts and uncles opined about our personalities or our competencies. Were we destined to be the engineer, the architect, the soldier, the priest, or the artist? Personally, I do not remember the counselor or the gerontologist as options!

Also, early in life, we have the conflict emerging between society's needs and the pursuit of our own passions. Many developing countries assume that their brightest young people will learn the skills of such professions as medicine, engineering, law, or education, so they can support the evolution and development of that particular society.

> Regardless of the venue of our labors, our work is an extremely important expression of who we are.

In my work with executives, I routinely encounter people who ended up in careers that were not totally of their choosing. Perhaps they were so smart that their parents and teachers assumed that they would become doctors or lawyers. Twenty years later, the angst may reveal itself in job dissatisfaction and relationship conflicts. Such was the case with the seminar participant I described in the preceding chapter.

Regardless of the venue of our labors, our work is an extremely important expression of who we are. The late John O'Donohue, in his beautiful book *Anam Cara*[1], reminded us that within each of us is a desire to be creative, to be a part of bringing forth something new and unique—to impart our unique essence.

Just look at what you do when you are not at the workplace. Observe how you express your creativity in your after-hours or weekend hobbies. Work best

> We seek environments where we can unleash creativity, passion, and potential—environments where potential becomes actual. Being able to describe that extraordinariness is to be able to describe the *soul* of the workplace you seek.

contributes to corporate achievement when it is designed to enhance individual self-actualization and to stimulate the expression of the full range of human talent and spirit.

Each of us has a particular gift to offer. Identifying that gift is the purpose of this chapter. Ideally, the workplaces we select should provide safe environments that satisfy our needs to belong and to do something extraordinary. We seek environments where we can unleash creativity, passion, and potential—environments where potential becomes actual. Being able to describe that extraordinariness is to be able to describe the *soul* of the workplace you seek.

ARE YOU SATISFIED WITH YOUR CAREER?

So did you choose the right career? Are you satisfied in your current position? Do you feel known, respected, listened to, and communicated with? Do you feel like you are a member of a profession? Are you able to express your extraordinariness?

Sadly, job dissatisfaction is widespread among workers of all ages and across all income brackets[2]. Significantly less than half of workers are satisfied with their jobs. The greatest dissatisfaction is among younger workers. It is not surprising that mockumentary and cringe comedy programs such as *The Office* are so popular. Real-life workplaces provide plenty of material. Managerial stupidity has now given way to an epidemic of bullying.

Job satisfaction is defined as a pleasurable emotional state resulting from the appraisal of one's job[3]. It derives from our feelings, our beliefs, and our behaviors. Not surprisingly, job satisfaction is correlated with life satisfaction. And the correlation is reciprocal.

The top expectations are for work that lets us feel that we have accomplished something meaningful, provides job security and steady employment, is with a reputable company, provides opportunities for advancement, is alongside competent and congenial coworkers, provides fair pay, appreciates the human qualities of supervision, demands reasonable hours, has meaningful benefits, and has safe working conditions.

Since the early 1920s, social scientists have been measuring the discrepancy between what we want in our jobs and what we have in our jobs. The prevailing wisdom is that certain job characteristics (skill variety, task identity, task significance, autonomy, and feedback) impact certain psychological states (experienced meaningfulness, experienced responsibility for outcomes, and knowledge of the actual results), which in turn impact work outcomes (job satisfaction, absenteeism, and work motivation).[4]

> What *doors* did you keep closed and what *doors* did you open?

When attempting to diagnose your job satisfaction, note that it may be intrinsic, relating to the kind of work you do and the tasks that make up your job; or it may be extrinsic, relating to the conditions of the work, such as pay, coworkers, or supervisor. It is important to look at these two separately. If you are concerned about the former, then you may need to consider a career change. In the case of the latter, you may be able to negotiate changes in the management style and culture of the company or the opportunities for employee involvement, empowerment, and autonomous work groups. You can do this by educating management about the **Third Circle** concept.

As an executive, you undoubtedly have a healthy amount of ambition and, as such, are pursuing your "Third Circle." But your "Third Circle" must be compatible with that of your superiors. Are you loyal to your superiors' goals? Is the situation satisfying to you?

I am a faithful reader each week of the *Economist* magazine. Not to sound morbid, but one of my favorite items is the obituary. The anonymous writer (although I heard her interviewed on National Public Radio) does a beautiful job of introducing us to her subject's life and accomplishments, as well as celebrating his or her rich and fulfilling life. Invariably, many subjects spent their whole lives dedicated to expanding our knowledge of a topic or advancing a meaningful cause. But there are others who began one place but, by virtue of the *doors* they chose to open or close, ended up far from their career origins.

Over the years I have worked with, or had line of sight to, many very successful leaders who made vital and constructive contributions well into their later years. To be sure, they took respites to rejuvenate themselves but were distinguished by the luxury of not separating work from play. How sad, in contrast, to watch so many executives agonize about the labor of their work and count the days until retirement. How might the *Economist* report on the accomplishments of your life? What *doors* did you keep closed and what *doors* did you open?

> Instead of building upon our unique essence, too often we define ourselves solely by the academic degrees we have earned or by the job titles we currently hold—ignoring many of the life experiences upon which we can build trusted and effective presences and contributions in our important relationships.

WHAT IS YOUR LIFE STORY?

Obviously the first adult step in the choice of a career or the confrontation of job dissatisfaction is to truly know oneself. Instead of building upon our unique essence, too often we define ourselves solely by the academic degrees we have earned or by the job titles we currently hold—ignoring many of the life experiences upon which we can build trusted and effective presences and contributions in our important relationships.

With every new leadership coaching assignment, the first thing I strive to discover is my client's life story. Where were they born and raised? Who raised them and initiated them into their culture of origin? What models did they have? Who sponsored or mentored them? What challenges were they faced with, and how did they handle them? These conversations are the most interesting aspect of my work—getting to truly *know* and understand the leader and his or her life's story.

Your life's story contains powerful information about the influences that have guided, and will continue to guide, your life. The first step in knowing yourself is to examine the people, places, and things that are prominent in your memory and serve as significant influences and defining moments.

> Your values—your non-negotiables—will set the trajectory for your career and give you the confidence and self-esteem to pursue your calling.

What aspects of your life's story would others benefit from knowing? What have you chosen or not chosen from your story to carry through your life? Who were your heroes as a child and why? How did they influence what *doors* you opened or closed?

WHAT DO YOU STAND FOR?

This is not to suggest that you should assert your religious or political views to others. Rather, it is to suggest that you should articulate the *soul* of your business and declare what, for you, is non-negotiable when it comes to your values and how you will live them strategically and through the execution of your work.

Values underlie our most important human concerns. Your values—your non-negotiables—will set the trajectory for your career and give you the confidence and self-esteem to pursue your calling. Leadership is like a vocation. A vocation begins with values, commitment, and sacrifice. It also brings peace of mind and the satisfaction that comes from a meaningful, other-directed life.

In order for this to occur, you must determine your own core values and then practice them. This is one of the most critical determinants of others' safeness, commitment, and morale. It is also the driver of trusted and effective leadership and the differentiator of the leader with "class." It is also the differentiator of the person with a "Third Circle."

Values form the culture of a marriage, a family, an organization, or a community and are reflected in a "Third Circle." Values also influence the courses of action taken to achieve these ends—that is, their strategies. Effectively, core values are a precondition for organizational excellence. As such, it is vital that core values are upheld by the entire organization, so all members are working together with a unity of purpose. By extension, belonging to the organization becomes the center of excellence and gives the organization a sense of identity. There is no strength without unity.

> Values form the culture of a marriage, a family, an organization, or a community and are reflected in a "Third Circle."

Because core values are intangible, it is tempting for leaders to focus on required competencies, goals, or results that can be readily identified. Unfortunately, core values are not the product of having the required competencies or even of having identified shared goals. Rather, core values reflect the leader's judgment as to what is meaningful or important in life and provide a yardstick against which personal, organizational, and societal behavior can be measured.

It is not enough for leadership to control, arrange, and "do things right." Leadership must unleash energy, set the "Third Circle," and do the right thing. Consequently, it is essential for you to hold a profound understanding of the values for which you stand. Understanding your life's story as well as your "Third Circle" will enable you to clarify your values. When you are certain and have a strong conviction of the moral worthiness of your beliefs and business purpose, you will be able to build these values into your employees and your organization as a whole.

Lastly, when I am coaching executives who are struggling with an ethical dilemma or with the choice between differing courses of action, I will persistently confront them with the question, "What do you know?" Invariably they know, deep in their hearts, what they stand for and should do. They know what actions match their values and the principles for which they stand. Sometimes, listening to what you already know is difficult amidst the noise and stress in which you live. But you cannot claim deferred ethics!

WHAT DO YOU HAVE TO LEVERAGE?

What do you do exceptionally well? You cannot build on quicksand. Yet many people either set themselves up to do so, or allow others to place them in positions that do not allow them to build upon the solid ground of that which they do exceptionally well. In the words of Thomas Carlyle, "Blessed is he who has found his work."

A trade not properly learned is an enemy. God forbid that you would be under the scalpel of a poorly trained surgeon! What is your sweet spot? People who are clear about their own strengths are better able to capitalize on their assets. This kind of awareness can lead to both individual effectiveness and personal growth. Further, it is important for trusted and effective leaders to reflect on their own personal progress and improvement—and to celebrate it by conveying it to others and rewarding themselves in some small way.

The first step in becoming trusted and effective, whether in personal or professional pursuits, is to truly know oneself. Besides understanding the impact of your life's story and the evolution of your value system, knowing your psychological makeup is imperative. As the Russian proverb reminds us, "There is no shame in not knowing; the shame is in not finding out."

I am often asked if I can psychometrically determine who will be a leader. While I can develop some insights in this regard, I can be more precise regarding who will *not* be a leader. If someone cannot sell a life jacket to a drowning person, it is unlikely that he or she will convince others to follow them. A few years ago I was asked to coach a senior executive in a major automobile company. This individual was clearly a candidate for the top job, but there was something missing. His extreme introversion compromised his ability to create a sense of safeness in others. When others experience us as difficult to get to know, feel they cannot read us or predict how we might act, or do not feel safe and secure in our presence, then it does not portend well for our leadership.

FINDING THE RIGHT CAREER

If truth be known, we probably knew very early in life what would give us the greatest career satisfaction. But that was before adults slammed the *doors* closed by telling us we were dreaming. To be sure, adults were our earliest mentors, but like teachers, they often discouraged our purposeful play. Is not play where children act out the work they love? Can you recall the substance of your childhood play? Did anyone slam a *door* shut on your dreaming? "Our senses are indeed our *doors* and windows on this world," wrote Jean Houston, an American author involved in the human potential movement, "in a very real sense the key to the unlocking of meaning and the wellspring of creativity."

How much exploration of different careers did you undertake before you committed to your career path? As I mentioned earlier, if we are academically bright we are often co-opted for one of the professions. Sometimes those professions are so demanding that we do not have the discretionary time to pursue our hobbies—those activities where we get to continue the play of our youth.

Whether you are in the mature stage of your career or renewing your exploration, it is useful to get to know yourself psychometrically. To be sure, certain personality traits and behavioral styles portend certain types of work. When mismatched, discomfort is felt. Most of the career-oriented psychometric instruments in use today are based on the work of John L. Holland, Ph.D[5]. As a classification interviewer with the United States Army, Dr. Holland realized that many people seemed to be examples of common personality types. This led to his formulation of the six basic categories in his person-environment typology.

The Holland Themes help people make career and educational choices that match their own interests and abilities. His theory provides an intellectual tool for integrating our knowledge of vocational intentions, vocational interests, personalities, and work histories. The Holland General Occupational Themes reflect six personality types: Realistic, Investigative, Artistic, Social, Enterprising, and Conventional. People of the same type tend to flock together. For example, Artistic types are attracted to making friends and working with other Artistic people. When Artistic types work together they tend to create a work environment that rewards creative thinking and behavior. Holland's theory presumes that people who chose to work in an environment similar to their personality type are more likely to be successful and satisfied.

> Do not underestimate, regardless of your place in the organizational structure, the importance of mentors, for they are the *door*-openers of both your mind and your affiliations.

Regardless of your temperament, force yourself to learn areas of substance that may not initially appeal to you. If you run a business, regardless of its size, you will have to balance the books. Modern companies are so complex that a disproportionate number of accountants ascend to their leadership when, in fact, what companies may need are more creative and innovative approaches to markets, products, and human capital.

Social scientists have for some time been curious about why some young men, raised in the most under-privileged environments, still find a way to break out and succeed both in life and business. Their conclusion is that such young men had significant male mentors at critical points in their development. Do not underestimate, regardless of your place in the organizational structure, the importance of mentors, for they are the *door*-openers of both your mind and your affiliations. As a newspaper's radio advertisement that I hear when I am in Ireland claims: "Before you make up your mind, open it!"

ROLE OF CHARACTER, PERSONALITY, AND BEHAVIOR IN CAREER SUCCESS

Besides knowing your social history and its impact on your feelings, myths, and biases, it is vital to know how your character, personality, and behavior impact your effectiveness as well as how others experience you.

> Character is non-negotiable; personality is largely physiological and electrochemical; behavior is the thing we are most likely to change.

Character, personality, and behavior are integral when evaluating the degree to which you are trusted.

In terms of job performance and productivity, personality may be more important than job satisfaction. While the link between job satisfaction and performance is thought to be spurious, both satisfaction and performance are the result of personality.

Invariably, my new clients refer to all people issues as "personality." They confuse character, personality, and behavior and refer to them as one. Character is non-negotiable; personality is largely physiological and electro-chemical; behavior is the thing we are most likely to change.

WHAT IS YOUR CHARACTER?

Character refers to individual differences in voluntary goals and values. These differences tend to be based on insights, intuitions, and concepts about oneself, other people, and other objects. Character indicates what we make of ourselves intentionally and is thought to begin developing at birth.

There are three dimensions of character: self-directedness, cooperativeness, and self-transcendence. Character assessment is a valuable tool given that low character scores, which reflect deficits in impulse control, empathy, and conscience, are associated with substance abuse and antisocial behavior. Conversely, an individual who is high on these three dimensions will display the ability to be effectual (for example, exercise self-control or work toward and achieve desirable goals); have integrity (for example, be truthful and sincere or follow through on promises and duties); and be committed to a greater good that transcends self instead of being self-absorbed (for example, is able to take into account the impact of one's actions on others in ways that demonstrate consideration for others)[6].

Parents, professors, and executives affect character and competency development by inducing the right amount of frustration within their children, students, and associates. It is through the resolution of this frustration that character is formed and ethical behavior developed.

> It is through the resolution of this frustration that character is formed and ethical behavior developed.

At the root of most human interactions is the assumption that it is possible to infer the mental processes of other people. This assumption is evident in countless domains of contact. For example, the testimony of witnesses in criminal trials, the use of proxies in opinion surveys, the interaction of couples in marital relationships, and indeed in corporate dealings with associates, colleagues, and competitors.

The inherent belief is that others' behavior is analogous to our own, and thus we presume (erroneously) that the other has utilized similar mental processes to arrive at that behavior. Further, individuals tend to weigh negative behavior more heavily in making character attributions. So be aware: a single negative behavior can neutralize or cancel out countless demonstrations of positive behavior. As a result, we may find ourselves making character assassinations based on one or two actions that do not accurately reflect the personalities and characters of our colleagues or associates.

WHAT IS YOUR PERSONALITY?

Personality refers to regularities and consistencies across contexts, over time, and between behavioral domains in the behavior of individuals over the course of their lives. Is the person who is dominant on the job also dominant at home? Is the person who is assertive today also assertive tomorrow, next month, and next year? Is the person who appears to be conscientious on a personality test actually conscientious when given the opportunity to behave in a conscientious way? The way in which people learn from experience and then adapt their feelings, thoughts, and actions is what characterizes their personalities. A personality trait is a distinguishing, relatively enduring way in which one individual differs from another.

WHAT IS YOUR BEHAVIOR?

Above, I suggested that personality is largely electrochemical and that the main ingredient that we can change is behavior. Does this mean we are stuck with our personalities and the personalities of our colleagues? Research suggests that while personality becomes more stable with time, it is an ever-evolving aspect of self that retains the potential for change[7]. As we age, we are thought to "become more like ourselves." There are four primary processes of change, however, that facilitate adjustment of personality traits. These include, responding to contingencies, watching ourselves, watching others, and listening to others.

Responding to contingencies (environmental socialization and expectations)—roles such as being a manager come with specific expectations and demands for appropriate behavior such as acting industrious, serious, stable, intelligent, fair-minded, tactful, and reasonable. Thus, a person who is impulsive by nature would be expected to set aside his or her preference to make snap decisions in order to be an effective manager. Over a long period of time, meeting these demands and absorbing the subsequent reinforcing responses would contribute to personality change.

Watching ourselves (reflecting on one's own actions or self-insight)—continuing with the above example, if an individual is newly appointed to the managerial role and subsequently begins behaving in a more detached manner or decreasing personal connection, they may see themselves as acting less friendly with subordinates, a change that they then interpret as lack of interpersonal connection, and perceive themselves as having diminished desire for sociability[8]. Likewise, when we become more self-directed at work, we are apt to become more self-directed with personal relationships and leisure activities.

Watching others (observational learning)—within the workplace, this type of change is facilitated most readily through mentorship between a senior member and a junior member of an organization in which the mentor demonstrates role-appropriate behaviors and how to behave effectively in the organizational setting. Outcome studies suggest that mentored individuals report higher levels of career success, greater satisfaction, better understanding of organizational norms and goals, and higher salaries than non-mentored individuals[9].

Listening to others (receiving feedback)—a significant source of information about ourselves and subsequently a potential source of change are the people with whom we interact and the feedback they provide us. It is thought that people develop meanings about themselves through feedback from others. Thus, when individuals receive new feedback concerning their personalities through employers, colleagues, or personal relationships, they may be more likely to change.

Erich Fromm observed, "Man's main task in life is to give birth to himself, to become what he potentially is. The most important product of his effort is his own personality." Unfortunately, in terms of empirical evidence, feedback has proven to be the least effective mode of personality change. This is because individuals often minimize or deny feedback that does not fit with their already developed self-concept. The most effective means for change include environment or system-wide changes that individuals must adapt to (for example, adjusting compensation packages to include metrics that are quality-related to help managers focus on quality), and a mentoring relationship or face-to-face contact with the immediate supervisor.

WHAT COULD SABOTAGE YOUR CAREER?

My years of experience coaching executives confirm that when we lose the trust of those we are leading, cannot cope with the stress of change, or do not have a "Third Circle," we are destined to derail and not survive otherwise successful careers. So how can we recognize and avoid those things that might derail our careers?

Would you feel safe with a boss who is living in the past, has stayed too long in a job he clearly dislikes, has tunnel vision, is burned out, neglects his personal health, has allowed his skills to atrophy, overreacts to problems, fails to plan, and is scared to take risks?

As we shall see in subsequent chapters, the relationships we have with our life partners, our children, our employees, our customers, and our fellow citizens profoundly impact our job satisfaction and effectiveness. Problems within any of those relationships will compromise our professional performances.

Would you feel safe with a boss who is living in the past, has stayed too long in a job he clearly dislikes, has tunnel vision, is burned out, neglects his personal health, has allowed his skills to atrophy, overreacts to problems, fails to plan, and is scared to take risks? When these symptoms persist, depression is probable. The best antidote to these symptoms is to reclaim the creativity to lead change with passion and vitality.

Over my years of watching employees and executives (remember career satisfaction is low across all ages and income levels) get burned out, I am painfully reminded of Sydney Pollack's 1969 movie *They Shoot Horses, Don't They?* Obviously, the title draws from the practice among horse owners of shooting a horse when it breaks a leg. It was considered humane to put the animal out of its misery, but it also alludes to the reality that it may have passed its usefulness.

Decades before *Jerry Springer* and *Survivor*, this movie focused on public competition and humiliation by using the setting of the sleazy and claustrophobic Depression-era dance marathons. Unemployed Americans participated in Social Darwinist exhibitions as a form of grunt labor for getting three meals a day. Pollack's film explores the depths to which self-destructive people will go when they are desperate. It is a fascinating and troubling film that spotlights the dark side of capitalism and memorializes a Depression-era fad that has fortunately faded away. Or has it?

> But since our economic security is so dependent upon having a job, the challenge is like trying to change suits while running full-out on a treadmill!

Too often, when we are dissatisfied with our work and are stressed-out, we become immobilized—like a deer in the headlights. We hit *The Wall.* Like personal health, career health also requires the ability to adapt, regroup, and reinvent ourselves. But since our economic security is so dependent upon having a job, the challenge is like trying to change suits while running full-out on a treadmill!

The older we are, the harder adaptation becomes. Ideally, we should reverse engineer our careers. What do you want to be doing in the latter part of your career? Many executives hope for the opportunity to serve on corporate boards. But, as we have seen lately, not all public company boards are as effective as they could be. In fact, the greatest job satisfaction tends to be within privately-held companies, and many of them are returning to a form of paternalism more familiar a few generations ago.

TAKE TIME TO STAND BACK AND REFLECT

The imagery of the treadmill reminds me of the 1960s musical *Stop the World—I Want to Get Off* by Leslie Bricusse and Anthony Newley. Ironically, it is set against the backdrop of a circus for a workplace. The protagonist, Littlechap, takes his first major step toward improving his lot by marrying his boss's daughter after getting her pregnant out of wedlock. Saddled with the responsibilities of a family, he allows his growing dissatisfaction with his existence to lead him into the arms of various women as he searches for something better than he has. He realizes, in the twilight of his life, what he always had—the love of his wife—to sustain him.

As I mentioned in the previous chapter, for over 20 years I have invited a small group of senior executives to attend my seminar "Trusted and Effective Leadership—Reclaiming the Creativity to Lead Change" at Ballynahinch Castle in the west of Ireland. To be sure, I am biased, but I have not yet found a comparable place in the world to be dropped off where my clients can "find their bliss," discover their personal "Third Circles" and courageously and intentionally imagine the "Third Circles" for their enterprises and for their lives. Perhaps Sedona, Arizona, approaches such a setting.

There are many wonderful castles in Ireland. Usually my clients from North America land, either privately or commercially, at Shannon. I advise them to first drop into Dromoland Castle (just north of the airport), breathe in the fresh Irish air after the Trans-Atlantic crossing, and then enjoy a traditional Irish breakfast.

I also recommend that they spend an evening in Galway city and experience the cultural heart of the west of Ireland. Besides enjoying incredible restaurants and street entertainment, they will hear the Irish language spoken, witness spontaneous gatherings of amateur musicians playing traditional Irish music in the pubs, and engage locals in some of the most stimulating conversations they may ever have. All of this before even getting to the castle!

Ballynahinch Castle is a renowned fishing hotel, forty miles west of the city of Galway, in the heart of Connemara, an area of outstanding natural beauty. It is now a crenellated Victorian mansion and enjoys a most romantic setting on 450 acres of ancient woodlands and gardens on the banks of the Ballynahinch River. Its scale is impressive, and the atmosphere is incredibly relaxed and truly magical.

The castle was built in the 1750s and was the original home of the "ferocious" O'Flaherty clan who lived there until the end of the century. One of the most notable residents was Grace O'Malley, the wife of clan member Donal O'Flaherty. Grace O'Malley was also known as Pirate Grace, as she was a pirate on the high seas around Ireland.

> It is unquestionably the perfect setting in which to stand back and reclaim the creativity to lead change.

The castle has seen many other distinguished owners since then, including "Humanity" Dick Martin (considered the founder of the Irish Society for the Prevention of Cruelty to Animals) and Prince Ranjitsinhji Maharajah of Nawanager (the famous and wealthy Indian cricketer). The castle offers three miles of private fly fishing for Atlantic salmon, sea trout, and brown trout. There are also 13,000 acres of prime woodcock shooting.

As part of our orientation to the castle we remind our clients that, while the modern amenities are nice, the setting is exquisite, the ambience is charming, and the service is out of this world, Ballynahinch and Connemara are also a model for how the people retained traditions against very difficult odds—something we expect successful business leaders to navigate despite the challenges they encounter in the business world.

Despite the billions of dollars my clients manage, or the ends of the earth to which their corporate jets take them, they confirm that they never enjoyed a place with the spirituality, tranquility, understated elegance, or cultural safety more than they experienced Ballynahinch. It is unquestionably the perfect setting in which to stand back and reclaim the creativity to lead change.

As I mentioned earlier, leadership is not about maintaining the status quo—it is about creatively leading change. Too often creativity is either stifled or never unleashed.

Not everyone I work with makes it to Ireland. Recently, I was able to direct one of my clients to a local option to meet his personal and spiritual needs.

This particular executive, Joe, expressed significant dissatisfaction with his work-life balance. It is important to know that Joe is an ordained minister, a lawyer by training and, at the time of our meeting, a senior vice president of human resources for a major United States public corporation. As we worked together, Joe concluded that what was most painful to him was the loss of the spiritual dimension in his life. He asked me if I could recommend an experience that might facilitate a healing process. I recommended a long weekend at Mepkin Abbey, a Trappist monastery in Berkley County, South Carolina. The abbey is located near Moncks Corner, at the junction of the two forks of the Cooper River northwest of Charleston.

Weeks passed without hearing from Joe. Then one morning, as I was driving north on Interstate 55 in Arkansas, my mobile phone rang. It was Joe announcing, "I am back!" "Back from where?" I asked. "From Mepkin Abbey," he proudly announced. "I signed up for a month!"

As he described his experience to me, I asserted that he needed to write down the experience from beginning to end. What he wrote was incredible.

His first impression was the profound silence. The monks at Mepkin are Cistercian, which means they are mostly a silent order given to contemplative prayer. They speak only when necessary to facilitate their work and during worship. Otherwise, they are completely silent. Joe quickly intuited that the goal while he was there was to allow the silence of the place to enter into him.

Only a few hours after arriving at Mepkin, however, he began to sense the beauty in the silence. There were approximately fifty people, including the twenty-nine monks, staying at the abbey. He found it amazing how silent they could all be even when they were in the same room eating their simple meals, passing in the stone corridors and the garden-like walkways, and sharing the plain four-bedroom cottages. There was no clanking of dinnerware, shuffling and scraping of chairs, no spoken words of greeting or otherwise. Every movement was made with great care and reverence for the silence. Doors and gates were opened and closed in a way to keep them from being heard. Each person unconsciously shifted their manner of walking to avoid making sounds with their shoes. It was this community of silence that quickly became proudly beautiful to him.

Part of Joe's fascination grew from the awareness that, even though they were silent, they were still constantly communicating. He swiftly learned to use his facial expressions and body movements to express his emotions and reactions, to convey grace and support, and to indicate relative degrees of importance. True, he was not attempting to explain physics or financial calculations, but he was surprised by how much he could "say" without words, and that what was "said" without words came across as embodying more goodwill than most conversations with words. He just seemed to work harder at being nicer to others.

> At the abbey, people were good enough at communicating without words that within a few days some of the visitors had bonded to varying degrees into a relatively close community.

It also seemed to him that the non-verbal language he was using—the expressions and other body language—was universally understood and needed no translation. Only later did he read that children born blind make the same facial expressions to communicate their feelings that those with sight use, which indicates there is something innate about this language. At the abbey, people were good enough at communicating without words that within a few days some of the visitors had bonded to varying degrees into a relatively close community. After leaving, he experienced this as a feeling of loss while he warmly remembered one of the older monks who showed him great kindness and affirmation—even though he never spoke a word to him!

As I reflect on his experience I am reminded of Spencer Tracy's advice to the young Burt Reynolds, "Less is more on screen."

Primarily, however, the beauty of the silence was in the growing effects it had on Joe's inner abilities to observe, reflect, find creative insights, and sense solutions for opaque problems. He later observed that these effects showed up most concretely in his journaling, which he had maintained for years. His entries during the stay at Mepkin were in marked contrast to those from earlier periods. They contained far more detailed descriptions, the reflections were to some degree more mature, and the insights were quantitatively more numerous and qualitatively more substantive. And the entries, when he was wrestling with a problem, evidenced more awareness. Joe was not claiming that he suddenly became a genius, only that he made marked progress in a relatively short period of time as a result of the silence.

> In most American corporations there is absolutely no importance attached, or time given, to the work of the subconscious.

Joe later joked with friends that he went to a silent monastery to "detox" from his experience in the corporate world. He noted that the modern corporate environment is obviously not a place of silence. Rather, it is one of constant, unrelenting pressure for higher performance. This creates a culture that demands the frantic pursuit of "flawless execution" by the "smartest people in the business." The worst thing that can happen to employees in such cultures is to be perceived as less than "all in" or anything less than among the "brightest." Week after week there is almost no time for contemplation that is free from the intense pressure, or from frequent interruptions and other distractions.

While recent research shows the pernicious effects of distractions, the problem, to Joe, runs deeper than that. In most American corporations there is absolutely no importance attached, or time given, to the work of the subconscious. In fact, it might be argued that the subject is never even considered, certainly not by executives. But it is becoming clear that the work of the subconscious mind is more important to success than generally believed. One example is that while higher IQ obviously offers many advantages, emotional intelligence (EQ) is no less important to overall success. Those with higher IQs are better at quickly choosing and applying known solutions to vexing problems, but those with higher EQs are better at quickly finding practical solutions when none are known.

The second impression Joe had from his time at Mepkin originated from those occasions when they did speak. Speaking and hearing took on greater significance and occurred in different ways. Though no one instructed them to do so, when each person spoke they effortlessly used an economy of words so that sentences were succinct and direct, but graciously intoned. Thus, in speaking they seemed to intuitively consider the message to be conveyed, the choice of words to be used, and the inflections that would convey the desired tone.

The more he tried to be aware of, and better understand, what he was experiencing when they spoke to one another, the impression deepened in him that the spoken word is rarely done well.

Joe found that as hearers they seemed to listen more thoughtfully, eager not only to comprehend the message of the words themselves, but also to gain some understanding of what the person was speaking to them. The more he tried to be aware of, and better understand, what he was experiencing when they spoke to one another, the impression deepened in him that the spoken word is rarely done well. Communicating is difficult, on any level. He learned that there are all kinds of misuses of the spoken word— like there are of the written word—but those that stood out in his mind related mainly to quantity, selection, message, and tone.

For example, Joe had ten minutes each day when he could call his wife. He and his wife approached these phone conversations from completely different perspectives. She wanted to share with him, her intimate confidant, the full load in all its excruciating details. He realized that, as we all do, she tended to start at the periphery and work her way slowly toward the central, most important matters. Conversely, he was in a serene place away from life's cares spending time in silent contemplation. And even though he was keenly interested in hearing everything on her mind, there was a part of him that wanted her to slow down, be more succinct, and start with the truly significant topics.

Besides being primarily materially focused, that lifestyle is uniquely egocentric and has resulted in the devaluing, and destruction, of the primary relational values that do bring happiness, meaning, and satisfaction, whether in the home or on the job.

In the corporate world, he often heard superiors talking to subordinates with language that was imprecise and conveying messages that were unclear in tones that were harsh if not downright disrespectful of others, and such conversations were frequently punctuated with crude expletives that were evidently intended to serve as whips to improve performance. He never believed or saw the slightest proof that conversations of this kind provided any benefits, but he did see plenty of evidence that their effects were entirely negative, both for the individuals involved and for the larger organization.

The third impression Joe had sprang from the worship assemblies that occurred seven times each day starting at 3:20 in the morning. Though the schedule was admittedly tiring on a physical level—at least partly, if not mainly, because he was not accustomed to it—the rhythm of each day quickly became spiritually meaningful and pleasurable to him. And the simple content and methodology of the assemblies served to strengthen the meaning. There was only one homily each week, and it was short, no more than ten minutes in length. They generally spent the whole time in each assembly (usually about an hour) reading or chanting selections of scripture and praying using selected scriptures.

The chief effect on him was a growing awareness that pursuing the dominant modern American lifestyle can never produce the happiness, meaning, and satisfaction that he desired most deeply. Besides being primarily materially focused, that lifestyle is uniquely egocentric and has resulted in the devaluing, and destruction, of the primary relational values that do bring happiness, meaning, and satisfaction, whether in the home or on the job. Research has shown that at a certain point happiness is not directly related to more money or more material possessions. Research has also shown that happiness is directly related to the number of long-term, deeply committed, trusting relationships one has. And the key to creating and maintaining such relationships is an unselfish commitment to the welfare of the other.

Unselfishness is a primary essential for human fulfillment. To Joe, all that is good for human beings will be found in self-sacrificing, self-giving relationships. As Zig Ziglar has said for years, "You can have everything in life you want, if you will just help enough other people get what they want."

To Joe, "fulfillment" and "happiness" are not synonymous with how "success" is determined in our culture. In fact, after spending time with monks who labor hard at living simple lives of daily contemplative prayer, he would advance the premise that such "success" will most often lead one to miss true fulfillment. But our culture of success is a powerful thing, and it keeps its hooks in us. Part of Joe wishes he could be a monk, cloistered in a monastery spending his days praying, but the one impression about which he had a high degree of certainty was that he was certainly no monk. He is too much a man of the culture around him.

DO YOU HAVE THE SELF-DISCIPLINE OF AN OLYMPIAN?

Your personal and leadership development will start when you acknowledge that you have not tapped into all of your potential, have not integrated all of your talents, but like an Olympic athlete, are open to personal and professional growth.

The comparison to the Olympian is quite appropriate. Most Olympic contestants these days are physiologically and biomechanically comparable. Besides innate ability or talent, the winner is different either by biochemical cheating or by superior coaching—coaching that helps the athlete visualize the superior execution of his or her ideal performance—his or her "Third Circle."

Two things are always clear. First, there was a lifetime of discipline behind the elegant performance. Second, the journey to greatness began very early in life. Have you had the same preparation to realize your "Third Circle"? Do you want to enjoy the rich success of *true* profitability or settle for mediocre power and a payoff that is cheaply gained? Remember, there is no luck except where there is discipline.

No one cares more about your career than you do. So take charge of it. Be intentional. These days, many executives retain the services of an executive coach who is trained to help the executives identify their unique talents and navigate the *doors* and *locks* to reach their "Third Circles." The more sophisticated coaches can also integrate the six pillars of *true* success and happiness.

Reflective Questions

■ What career did you imagine yourself having when you were young? Are you pursuing that career today?

■ What is your professional "Third Circle"? Where do you want to be tomorrow, in one year, in five years, by retirement?

■ What have been the hardest or most challenging events in your career, and how did you cope with them?

In truth, the life story of a family, across all its generations, is the story of who did or who did not achieve their personal "Third Circles" or the "Third Circle" for a relationship.

CHAPTER 4

Then, Companionship

When there is love in a marriage, there is harmony in the home; there is contentment in the community; there is prosperity in the nation; when there is prosperity in the nation, there is peace in the world. *—Chinese proverb*

While your career may be the first important choice you make, the choice of your life companion is by far the most important decision you will ever make. Yet it is a decision to which most people give too little thought. Too often the selection is purely emotional rather than intentional. It is not surprising then that so much of the decision is based on chance.

Research into the phenomenon of trust reveals that, regardless of our academic or financial accomplishments, we are generally predisposed to trust others, often to a fault. We approach many people and situations without a healthy amount of skepticism. Because of our biases we are often poor judges of people and situations. Our exquisitely adapted, cue-driven brains may, therefore, be vulnerable to exploitation by all kinds of people in our lives, not to mention possible suitors.

We see what we want to see, known as confirmation bias, and consequently our presumptions overweigh the supporting evidence about our decision.

Further, we are heavily influenced by the social stereotypes we have. We may link observable cues such as facial characteristics, age, gender, or race with psychological traits such as honesty, reliability, or trustworthiness.

Are you capable of being intentional when it comes to selecting a life partner? Would you board an airplane when there is only a 50 percent chance of it reaching its destination? Such is the fate of first-time marriages in the United States today. In the words of Goethe: "Love is an ideal thing, marriage a real thing."

> Would you board an airplane when there is only a 50 percent chance of it reaching its destination?

Our natural (and unrealistic) inclination to be optimistic can result in us overestimating that good things will happen—for example, that we will marry well, have successful careers, live long lives, and so forth—despite information about the odds that would suggest the contrary. The reality is that each of us must work hard at marriage, career, child-rearing, and health maintenance.

In truth, this chapter reflects my own life biases. While the chapter will largely refer to life partnerships between a man and a woman, I believe that the **Third Circle** concept is equally applicable to any life partner relationship that involves commitment with the potential to produce something beautiful. That commitment may be to the priesthood, a marriage, parenthood, a lover, a companion, or a friend. My intention is to advance the appreciation of diversity in all of its dimensions and in all of its settings. If you are in a same gender relationship, have a special friendship, or have a responsibility you had not planned on, please assume that when I refer to *life partner*, I am also speaking to you.

THE WRONG CHOICE IS VERY COSTLY!

The effects upon the workplace from an employee being distracted by a domestic relationship problem are highly predictable. Productivity and quality decline; his or her poor attitude rubs off on co-workers who have to pick up the slack; productivity declines across all employees; customer service suffers; product quality drops; sales decline; and the bottom line takes a hit. Typically, there are excessive absences due to stress or illness, as well as work interruptions for meetings with accountants, attorneys, counselors, teachers, and judges. When the employee is physically at work, he or she may not be emotionally present. Besides the economic costs associated with this level of disengagement, there may also be serious safety issues depending on the particular profession.

Regardless, a wrong choice will exert its impact on the effectiveness of your career, the quality of your parenting, the believability of your leadership, and the perceptions of your friends and customers. As with each of the critical relationships that impact *true* success and happiness, it is highly dependent upon trust, can be very stressful, and is destined to fail if there is not a "Third Circle" for the union.

> Is there a "Third Circle" for your marriage or relationship?

The professional counselors in my company are struck by how often they are working with two married people who are operating from two entirely different "Third Circles." As Zig Ziglar, the legendary motivational speaker, observed, "Many marriages would do better if the husband and the wife clearly understood that they are on the same side." Is there a "Third Circle" for your marriage or relationship?

OPENING THE DOOR TO YOUR FIRST CIRCLE

An unhealthy or unfulfilled relationship is often characterized by issues of trust, debilitating stress, isolation, and a sense of hopelessness. There may also be health problems such as depression, anxiety, chronic pain, and even curtailed longevity. The harder to measure effects, however, are the consequences of being distracted from your leadership responsibilities, be they as a parent, a manager, a vendor, or a politician. All of these impact your likelihood of being trusted and promoted.

My clients usually have some idea of how they would like their lives and their relationships to be, but they bring all of their collective stuff—all the physical, emotional, and cultural deficits and strengths. How they have coped with or grown from these experiences is reflected in their innate resiliency. As George Washington observed, "I have always considered marriage as the most interesting event of one's life, the foundation of happiness or misery."

Remember, your "First Circle" is characterized by pain and/or desire. Moreover it is frequently characterized by failures, incompetence, wishful thinking, and the repetition of unsuccessful attempts to relate to one another. Are you at risk of choosing or becoming the wrong mate?

Too many couples wait too long to open the *door* to obtaining the correct diagnoses about their relationships. They may be frustrated by the futility of past attempts to meet the ideal partners or to maintain domestic harmony. Remember that, as within the human body, pain is often referred, meaning that it may be felt some distance from where it is originating. So it is in relationships. Psychosomatic research repeatedly points to the emotional origins of so many physical symptoms that compromise the effectiveness of a partner to participate in the relationship. In the next chapter we will see how a failure in the early development of the emotional architecture of our minds can set us up for all kinds of problems in the critical relationships we are exploring in this book.

Do you have the maturity for marriage and commitment? Can you make another person feel safe?

After the initial euphoria, a couple may soon realize that they do not know each other and are attempting to build on a weak foundation. For example, their motivation to marry may be based exclusively on sex drive, the impending birth of a child, the woman's biological clock, or control issues within one or both partners. Worse still is the feeling of being trapped in an unhealthy, destructive relationship. A poor marriage can be a painfully lonely place.

How well do you know yourself? Do you have the maturity for marriage and commitment? Can you make another person feel safe? Too many people embark on marriage with extremely naïve assumptions. They are almost child-like, immature and clinging, assuming that others will make them happy. What expectations do you bring to the dating process or to a marriage? As John Barth, the legendary minister, noted, "Marriage is our last, best chance to grow up."

Too often people do not enter the relationship with a clean slate. They may still have romantic ties to previous soul mates. They may even bring disease. Or they may constantly refer to previous relationships. They may be bitter, hurt, or angry. What events in your life's story are likely to jeopardize your ability to commit to another person? Was your childhood abuse-free? What values are important to you? Emotional maturity is so essential for a healthy relationship. Do you come with baggage or as damaged goods? Are you possessive and jealous? Do you bring children with you? Are you part of the generational curse of divorce? Did you receive pre-marital training?

How well do you know the person you are thinking of choosing as your life partner or the person to whom you are already committed? Eleanor Roosevelt observed that "you never know anyone until you marry them." Do you make them feel safe both physically and emotionally or are you self-centered? What is the significance of the cultural or family backgrounds you each come from? Do you understand the differences between you and your partner? Do you share the same values, dreams, and commitment?

Are you and your partner capable of demonstrating respect to one another, or is your relationship characterized by constant arguments and nagging? There is a difference between quarreling that helps you get to know each other better and the cruel undermining of your partner's self-esteem and dignity. Gandhi humorously informed us that he learned the concepts of non-violence in his marriage. Is there equality within your marriage? Are your respective roles clearly understood and accepted? How well do you listen? Are you truly *in* the relationship or are you checking out through work, hobbies, or friends?

Poor communication is considered to be the greatest saboteur of any relationship. Good communication presumes listening, respect, and knowing. Communication is the currency through which the business of the marriage is conducted. It is through our communication skills that we resolve conflicts, solve problems, and sell our "Third Circles" to one another and to people outside the marriage. It is how dreams are shared.

> It is through our communication skills that we resolve conflicts, solve problems, and sell our "Third Circle" to one another and to people outside the marriage. It is how dreams are shared.

What attracts a potential life partner to you? Will these attributes sustain vitality within the relationship? Can you be trusted? A good marriage is largely good luck in finding the right person at the right time. The rest is trust.

How well do you adapt to change, or do you fail to cope with life's trials? Have you learned to be helpless? What are your personality traits, and how do they differ from those of your partner? How do you typically behave? Can others trust your character? Lillian Hellman, the American playwright, reminds us that "people change and forget to tell each other." Can you modify your behavior to make your partner feel safe? Do you have overboard habits, such as gambling, drugs, or violence?

Another major "First Circle" problem is the tension financial concerns place on a marriage. Do you comprehend your financial responsibilities?

Do you have the will to stick with a relationship? The author Pat Conroy lamented that "each divorce is the death of a small civilization." Do you still have hope that the ideal you envisioned when you embarked upon the relationship with your partner is attainable? Do you have a realistic vision for family life? Sadly, society no longer respects the sacredness of marriage. Do you have a support system of family and friends? Be aware that marriages are at the greatest risk after the birth of a second child or in the sixth year of the marriage.

Can you recall the initial spark that brought you and your partner together? What are you doing to retain the romance in your relationship? Diane Sollee, founder and director of Smart Marriages, challenges us that "to get divorced because love has died is like selling your car because it has run out of gas." In my home study I have pinned up a faded column by Billy Graham that I cut out from the *Charlotte Observer* many years ago. It is the evangelist's response to a letter and is entitled "True love is far deeper than just an emotion."

If you did not like your answers to these questions, do not despair; it is just where you are in your "First Circle." Being aware is the starting point. Now the work begins!

WHO IS YOUR IDEAL LIFE PARTNER?

Discoveries come to prepared minds. Benjamin Disraeli, a British prime minister during Queen Victoria's reign, noted that "the great secret in life is for a man to be ready when his opportunity comes." This applies to every dimension of life. Successful couples are able to describe their ideal partners. They can do this with conviction and without the typical trite platitudes.

Ultimately, success is characterized by a couple's compatibility across the life span. Who do you want to be with when you are 80 years of age? Robert Browning wrote, "Grow old along with me! / The best is yet to be, / The last of life, for which the first was made."

The "Third Circle" for your marriage will have integrity, reflected in the trust you have in one another; proportionality, reflected in the balance the relationship enjoys; and beauty, reflected in the daily pleasures you

The "Third Circle" for your marriage will have integrity, reflected in the trust you have in one another; proportionality, reflected in the balance the relationship enjoys; and beauty, reflected in the daily pleasures you share with each other.

share with each other. It will be a safe place, where the safeness is derived from the mutual admiration and commitment to be for each other and for the marriage. "My heart is ever at your service," wrote William Shakespeare. There will be a shared spiritual center. Those who reach their "Third Circles" do not settle for less than the ideal. But do not confuse wasting time looking for the perfect lover with creating the perfect love. As John O'Donohue admonished us, "Do not confuse glamour for beauty."

The pragmatic definition of marriage is that it is a partnership. Partnerships usually infer equality of ownership while capitalizing on the unique and different talents each partner brings to the union. Marriages also solve problems. Couples are constantly being presented with problems to solve. These may be around finances, the home, children, education, life situations, and so forth.

A colleague in my company was working with a couple who wanted to stop the overspending loop into which they had become trapped. She introduced them to the **Third Circle** concept. The couple met while they were in medical school and although their earning potential was great they quickly got in over their heads with a lifestyle that was beyond their means. Approximately three years after beginning in practice they sold their multi-million dollar home in a short sale and closed their two medical practices due to bankruptcy. They moved to a more affordable home and committed to a more low-key lifestyle with a less stressful life.

During counseling they conceded that it was a major struggle to change their approach to money. My colleague drew the "Third Circle" model, emphasizing what they had identified as their "First Circle," including the pain of losing their home and practice, the shame they felt, and their strong desire to not repeat the same mistakes.

With her help, they were able to identify the "Third Circle" for their lives, and for raising their children, with reduced worry and stress about money. They developed a skeleton plan for paying off family members who had loaned them money and some of the bills that were not covered by the bankruptcy proceedings. What they had not done was to expose their "saboteurs" or to identify what they had to "leverage." Their plan was weak and it was also open to sabotage.

My colleague worked diligently on identifying the saboteurs and reframing each of their approaches to money and spending. She processed with them what it felt like for the wife to be constrained to a budget when she had grown up with a father who doted on her with material things. For the husband, there was a desire to see her happy, but he resented the level of debt that he perceived was attributed to her over-spending.

Once they were able to expose these issues they were better able to put them to rest. They discussed how to leverage their commitment to each other, the power of listening, and positive communication. They revisited what had drawn them together in the first place, which had nothing to do with money or material things. In this way they were able to create a more realistic and honest plan to live a life without the pressure of debt.

They met with an accountant and a financial planner and for the first time moved into the adult role of saving for future needs and contingencies rather than spending with no thought. Previously they had been fearful of meeting with anyone to honestly discuss their money issues. With the commitment not to repeat their previous pain, by exposing their saboteurs and by leveraging their commitment and communication they were able to move toward their "Third Circle" for the first time in years. One year after doing this exercise, my colleague was happy to report that they had completely changed their approach to spending, had bought a house that was within their means, and were saving for their children's educations and their own retirement. They reported a greater honesty in their marriage and increased intimacy.

What can you not live without in a relationship? What do you need to thrive? What do you need each day from your partner? Can you ask your partner for what you need? So many couples assume that their partners can read their minds. Like our children, we can get stuck emotionally. In truth, the life story of a family, across all its generations, is the story of who did or who did not achieve their personal "Third Circles" or the "Third Circle" for a relationship. What *doors* did they open? What *doors* did they keep closed?

A healthy marriage is also characterized by good "ego" strength. "Ego" is frequently misunderstood, at least in the way that Freud intended. It is often confused with being "egotistical." Ego strength is best understood in terms of solving problems or dealing with life's frustrations. Persons, couples, or marriages that are high in ego strength tend to exhibit a stoic mental orientation. They accept that effort, frustration, and loss are inevitable parts of life. They avoid unrealistic expectations. They formulate problems in concrete and specific terms; then they reframe the problem in common-sense language. They also have an appropriate sense of timing, being neither hurried nor slow-paced. They do not procrastinate, nor do they try to comply with superhuman standards. They have positive self-images and can correctly discern the limits of their own control or responsibility. Finally, they prepare for stressful events by rehearsing for them.

> Watching a couple combine love and skill in the creation of a safe place for their children, their parents, and those close to them, to progress with dignity through their particular stage of life, is truly priceless.

Healthy problem solvers pass through four stages. First, they stoically define the facts; second, they creatively explore all the options available to solve the problem; third, they select an option that does not create another problem; and fourth, they act upon their decision. Couples who are highly effective problem solvers move through this sequence, almost imperceptibly, reading each other's minds. The confidence that results from this competence is ego strength. Reactive problem solvers, in contrast, see only one option, do not like it, cannot make a decision, and cause chaos for others around them, including their children, their employees, and their customers.

Watching a couple combine love and skill in the creation of a safe place for their children, their parents, and those close to them, to progress with dignity through their particular stage of life, is truly priceless.

Couples who reach their "Third Circles" are constantly learning and growing and reinventing their "Third Circles." They are givers not takers. They respect what they have created together: their home, their children, their traditions. They are good friends.

LEVERAGING YOUR STRENGTHS TO ATTRACT YOUR IDEAL PARTNER

John Fischer, a senior writer for the *Purpose Driven Life* website, reminds us: "The success of marriage comes not in finding the *right* person, but in the ability of both partners to adjust to the *real* person they inevitably realize they married." They learn how to deal with incompatibility and turn it into strength. They create intimacy.

> "There is nothing stronger in the world than gentleness."

Sometimes the executives I coach have difficulty thinking about intimacy in a business context. They would like to compartmentalize their lives. But true leaders are well-integrated people. They are consistent within and among the various domains of their lives. Moreover, they are very comfortable with intimacy. I frequently recommend that my Type A, driven executives watch how Dr. Han Suyin (played by Jennifer Jones) reminds Mark Elliott (played by William Holden) in the 1955 movie *Love is a Many-Splendored Thing* that "there is nothing stronger in the world than gentleness."

When we feel intimate with someone, we feel safe. We feel that we will not be harmed. To be sure, it can be an extremely fragile condition, for intimacy is the ultimate relationship. It depends on exquisite communication; undistracted listening; honor and respect for the other person; and an all-consuming desire to know the other person.

KNOW YOURSELF AND YOUR PARTNER

"What manner of a man is it that I have married?" exclaimed Mary Kate Danaher (played by Maureen O'Hara) about Seán Thornton (played by John Wayne) in the 1952 John Ford movie *The Quiet Man*.

How well do you know the person you are thinking of taking as a life partner? More importantly, how well do you know yourself? Do you understand the influence that your family of origin has upon the quality of the commitment you are prepared to make? What is the impact of your biases and prejudices on how you view a suitor?

> The worst thing you can do is to select someone as your partner who is morally untidy and whose character is unreliable, for relationships are based upon trust.

Start by letting go of the past. Discard the baggage of resentments, hurts, and fears towards anyone who was either a role model or participated directly in a relationship with you. Take inventory of how you act in relationships. If your past relationships did not work, you were probably 50 percent responsible. Do you understand why? Do you trust too readily or are you too mistrustful? Recognize, honor and pursue your needs. Choose a partner who will meet your long-term needs, not your short term wants.

Invest in the services of a psychologist or counselor who can help you know yourself, your motivations, and your needs. Recall, from chapter 3, that there is a difference between personality, behavior, and character. Compatibility does not mean that you and your partner are alike. It means that you complement each other. It is hard to change personality since it is largely physiological and electrochemical. Do not be naïve about your ability to change your partner's personality. We can change our behaviors if someone gets our attention. The worst thing you can do is to select someone as your partner who is morally untidy and whose character is unreliable, for relationships are based upon trust.

There are several compatibility testing services available to help you know yourself and a prospective partner. Be aware, however, that the assessments are fairly basic. They may get you in the ballpark with a prospect, but dig deeper if you are serious about a particular candidate.

DEMONSTRATE AND EXPECT RESPECT

There are two descriptions of respect. The first is the respect that is due to someone of particular standing and is often imposed through the exercise of power. In this case, you may think people respect you when, in fact, they fear you. If you focus on exercising power over your partner, you can damage the ability to enjoy true intimacy. Further, if your partner feels coerced into participation in the relationship, he or she may end up resenting you and the marriage, with the resultant loss of effectiveness of the partnership.

The second kind of respect is based on regard and attention. This kind of respect begins when each party believes that they have something to learn from the other. It requires both an awareness of one's own self-identity and an acceptance of other people's self-identities. Respect allows for consciousness raising, shared power, and inclusion. Note that respecting another individual does not necessitate always agreeing with him or her; rather, it involves engendering a feeling that he or she is important, and that his or her ideas are valued. Time after time, research confirms that respect is vital for true dialogue.

Too often there is a superficiality of respect during courtship. It is important that you develop and honor your own boundaries and those of your partner. The wrong person will cross your boundaries fairly early into the relationship. As Kahlil Gibran, the Lebanese-American artist, poet, and writer, observed: "Let there be spaces in your togetherness."

If you are seeking the ideal life partner, then redefine socializing. Socialize in a way that creates a rich, satisfying life and as a way to create a supportive, vibrant community. When your life works and you are happy, the right partner will be drawn to you.

THE FIRST DUTY OF LOVE IS TO LISTEN

Paul Tillich, the theologian and Christian existentialist philosopher, insists, "The first duty of love is to listen." The love interests who listen to us are the ones we move toward. When we are listened to, it creates us, makes us unfold and expand.

When our life partners listen to us, trust, motivation and participation are enhanced. Listening is an active process in which the listener enlists the skill of physical hearing as well as the skill of critically detecting nuances of language, including those of body and word. It requires paying attention as well as asking for input. Through listening, our partner is given the space to articulate his or her ideas and concerns, which will allow his or her perspective to be understood. Listening conveys that we value our partners' unique perspectives. Moreover, it enables us to become skillful conversationalists, to inquire about topics that are of importance to our partners, and to convey a message of caring.

> Listen to your partner so that he or she cannot possibly doubt that you love them.

There are four distinct listening styles: people-oriented, action-oriented, content-oriented, and time-oriented. A people-oriented listening style is characterized by a concern for others' feelings and emotions; this type of listener attempts to find areas of common interest with others. Action-oriented listeners prefer to receive concise, error-free presentations; disorganized presentations tend to frustrate the action-oriented listener. Content-oriented listeners are able to carefully evaluate facts and details before forming judgments and opinions and prefer complex and challenging information. Finally, time-oriented listeners tend to let others know how much time they have to listen and often have brief or hurried interactions.

No style is considered superior; what is important for successful life partnering, however, is to understand your own listening preferences as well as the listening preferences of your partner. Be careful to adjust your listening style when moving from work to home. Your life partner will not welcome being treated like an employee. David Augsburger, a minister of the Menonite Church and a pastoral counselor whose works revolve around the subjects of Christianity, hatred, prejudice, violence, and forgiveness, notes that "being heard is so close to being loved that for the average person, they are almost indistinguishable." Knowing what to listen for and how to listen facilitates effective communication. Listen to your partner so that he or she cannot possibly doubt that you love them.

MARRIAGE IS ONE LONG CONVERSATION

Someone once observed that marriage is not a word; it is a sentence. But it is often checkered with disputes, as Robert Louis Stevenson observed. Friedrich Nietzche, the nineteeth-century German philosopher, challenges us: "When marrying, ask yourself this question: do you believe that you will be able to converse well with this person into your old age? Everything else in marriage is transitory." Communication is an integral component for building trust and safeness in any relationship but is particularly important for domestic harmony. Sometimes you may have to question your partner to fully know a situation or the impact of a choice or a decision. Questioning a person you trust can be psychologically uncomfortable and anxiety producing. Frame your question as information seeking rather than as absolutes or personal attacks.

Scholars in the field of verbal communication usually use the term "verbal" in the strict sense, meaning "of or concerned with words," and do not use "verbal communication" as a synonym for oral or spoken communication only. Thus, sign languages and writing are generally understood as forms of verbal communication. Nonverbal communication is usually understood as the process of sending and receiving wordless messages. Such messages can be communicated through gesture; body language or posture; facial expression and eye gaze; object communication such as clothing, hairstyles, or even architecture; symbols and infographics; prosodic features of speech, such as intonation and stress; and other paralinguistic features of speech, such as voice quality, emotion, and speaking style.

Couples use all of these methods of communication both in their destructive form as well as in good partnering. I recently heard a visiting missionary from Kenya remind a congregation that the tongue is a very small part of the body, but it is capable of incredible destruction.

Conversely, a couple with an effective partnership uses communication to advance the business of their marriage, raise emotionally healthy children, and move in and out of a variety of social settings. As Robert C. Dodds, who was a former official of the National Council of Churches and also a psychologist and marriage counselor, reminds us, "The goal in marriage is not to think alike, but to think together."

> Conversely, a couple with an effective partnership, uses communication to advance the business of their marriage, raise emotionally healthy children, and move in and out of a variety of social settings.

When we use the word communicate, we are referring not only to the words we use to transfer factual information to our partners, but also to other "messages" that we send and receive. In fact, experts estimate that as much as 90 percent of what we communicate is nonverbal. Of late, my wife, Mary Pat, and I have become acutely aware of one form of non-verbal communication that borders on telepathy! On a recent visit to family and friends in England and Ireland, we both found ourselves making an observation only to have the other remark, "I was just thinking the same thing!" Approaching 40 years of marriage, we have a long history of shared memories, homes, traditions, values, experiences, possessions, friends, and goals. As Bill Cosby reminds us, "The heart of marriage is memories."

Communication is effective when a concise and clear message is delivered well, received successfully, and understood fully. Again, my wife is extremely effective in this regard. Probably the best example of her succinctness occurred one Saturday morning on the sideline of a soccer match in which our son, Seán, was playing. I was proposing something to which she was adamantly opposed. Borrowing from the first President Bush, and inspired by her orthodontist, she commanded, "Read my braces!"

Through your words, actions, body language, voice tone, you send many messages about yourself. This constitutes precisely one-half of the communication process. The second half consists of verifying that the message you intended to send was actually received and interpreted the way you intended. The only way that you can be sure you have created understanding is to listen to your partner and make special effort to encourage him or her to reflect back to you what he or she has heard, and what they make of it.

Remember that although you communicate in a way that seems clear to you, your partner is likely to filter the information through a very complicated set of preconceptions that can function to distort the message received. Also, receivers listen selectively. They hear and process some things and gate out other things. That means that while you may have explained the "whole picture," it is likely that the whole thing was not received. To confirm that you have created a common understanding with your partner ask him or her to repeat back what he or she heard and what his or her reactions are to your message. As the old saying goes, "No man is truly married until he understands every word his wife is not saying."

NO ROAD IS LONG WITH GOOD COMPANY

So goes the Turkish proverb. To be sure, the world revolves on the quality of relationships. If you are to find and sustain a lasting life partner relationship, you may need to develop new relationship patterns to replace your old ineffective ones. Friedrich Nietzsche also taught us that "it is not a lack of love, but a lack of friendship that makes unhappy marriages." There is no need like the lack of a friend.

Rich personal and professional relationships always have a subtle component of friendship. Friendship, unlike such institutions as marriage and parenthood, carries no legal bond or obligation. They grow incrementally and endure because of a delicate balance of acceptance

> When one friend is more demanding than the other, and takes more emotionally from the relationship, the friendship will collapse.

and support. When one friend is more demanding than the other, and takes more emotionally from the relationship, the friendship will collapse. There is an axiom in the psychology of friendship that states: I cannot promise that I will not hurt you; but it will not have been on purpose.

But people have great difficulty forgiving in both their personal and their professional lives. Many believe that they cannot put back together a crystal glass that has been broken. Yet forgiveness is one of the most interesting areas in health psychology, for the lack of forgiveness is very costly to our health. As Ruth Bell Graham, the late wife of the evangelist Billy Graham, observed, "A good marriage is the union of two good forgivers."

The resistance to forgive is a very primitive instinct that appears to be hard-wired within our psyches. If offended by someone, we tend to want to hurt them back. Quickly we get hooked, oscillating between the "Second" and "Third Circles." Forgiving requires us to convince ourselves that the hurt never happened. This can be very difficult, but being able to forgive is equivalent to giving ourselves a gift, clearing our hearts and minds of the poison of anger and resentment. Forgiving does not mean that we condone the hurtful event; rather we do not set ourselves up to seek revenge rather than justice, or elevate our obstinacy to a virtue. Being able to forgive is not an event in itself. Instead it can be a long process that is often aided by conversation with a friend.

True friends own an understanding of what it takes to sustain trust. Sometimes that may require making an apology. An appropriate apology includes the supplicant taking ownership of the violation (I was a real jerk, I really wasn't listening); expressing understanding of the emotional impact of the offense on the other person (I know I embarrassed you); expressing deep regret in a way that shows some humbling (I am really, really sorry), where the tone of voice matches the words; an attempt to explain the reasons behind the behavior (I was jealous, I was distracted); and expressing intent not to have the offense recur (I will do everything possible to make sure this does not happen again).

Sadly, there are those occasions when a broken relationship cannot be restored as well as we would like. Distance, death of one party, or just the unwillingness or lack of ability may make reconciliation untenable or a bad idea. In these cases, breaches in a close relationship remain as trauma. These unresolved or unhealed traumas can be the most powerful in creating future bias or resistance to forgiveness and trust in people. These wounds become the barriers to trusted and effective relationships.

Fortunately, the science of human behavior has a relatively new field, critical incident recovery. We have also learned much from the field of human grief work. The knowledge from both these areas of human behavior has taught us that we are hard-wired, even after brokenness and trauma, to move on with our lives. We can even claim some wisdom and depth from the pain, which can often shape us into deeper, wiser people.

So strengthen your faith and your trust in a universal source. Your faith is the one thing that you *can* count on. It gives you confidence. Moreover, it helps you avoid going back into unhealthy relationships. Develop a new set of dating relationships. Lay the foundation to attract a healthy life partner. Move slowly and spend quality time interacting with potential suitors.

Can you see the ideal relationship in your mind's eye? What is your ideal self? Where are you living? What are you doing for a living? Who is your life partner? How are your children doing? What are you passionate about? Does your partner help you in the expression of your unique essence through the work you do? Do you provide the same support for him or her?

WHAT COULD SABOTAGE YOUR RELATIONSHIP?

Sadly, the divorce rate in the United States is the highest in the world. Fifty percent of first marriages end in divorce, and 67 percent of second marriages fail. The effects of divorce are obvious in family life, educational attainment, job stability, income potential, physical and emotional health, drug use, and crime. Divorce is associated with depression as people experience the loss of a partner, their hopes, and their dreams—the loss of their "Third Circle." Often it is a prolonged, agonizing process of months to years.

> Create community, starting with your spiritual anchor, your partner, your family, your friends, your colleagues, and those who depend on your talents.

Outside the home, marital problems affect relationships with other family members, as well as friends, co-workers, and employers. Preoccupation with marital problems or the anxiety over a pending or ongoing breakup is certain to affect job performance. Women initiate divorce twice as often as men, but men are usually confronted with more emotional adjustment problems.

Divorce is as complex a problem as anyone is likely to face—much more complex than the business decisions we may be expected to make as executives. As with any change, there are stages through which the couple traverses on their way to divorce. Typically, these include the disillusionment of one or both parties, an expression of dissatisfaction, the decision to divorce, acting on the decision, a growing acceptance, and eventually, new beginnings. If you find yourself embarking upon such a journey, seek professional help to evaluate why the relationship is collapsing and to use the **Third Circle** concept to reset your life and inoculate yourself against the same issues that resulted in the loss of your current relationship.

If you can see your "Third Circle" for the perfect relationship, what are you prepared to confront? How are you prepared to change?

As with each of the relationships highlighted in this book, a problem within any one has the potential to contaminate each of the others. So examine your ability to commit, forgive, and fight fairly with a suitor, a partner, a child, a colleague, your employees, or your clients. Go beyond forgiveness and give. What does that look like?

Address the fear of failure and the fear of success that keep you trapped within your "First Circle." Know yourself. Know others. Preserve your personal and financial capital. Create community, starting with your spiritual anchor, your partner, your family, your friends, your colleagues, and those who depend on your talents. We live in each others' shelters. Unleash your creativity; for creativity is the most important talent that the loss of trust, stress, and personal drifting destroys.

DO YOU HAVE THE DISCIPLINE TO MAKE A RELATIONSHIP WORK?

This is the heart of this book. Relationships are all about commitment. Can you affirm your commitment to your life partner? If not, there is little hope that you will be a credible parent or a corporate leader who can orchestrate safeness within your employees and customers.

Warren Buffett notes that "when people tell me they've learned from experience, I tell them the trick is to learn from other people's experience." Consult with people who have stayed committed, despite the stresses, temptations, and distractions. Revisit the "First Circle" discussion and take inventory and invest in professional help. Such intentionality is no different than the risk management approaches you take with other areas of your life and business.

> Such intentionality is no different than the risk management approaches you take with other areas of your life and business.

Take heart from the words of the poet Homer: "There is nothing nobler or more admirable than when two people who see eye to eye keep house

as man and wife, confounding their enemies and delighting their friends."
True companionship!

Reflective Questions

■ What can you not live without in a relationship?

■ What about your partner did you fall in love with?
When did you know it? How strong is that aspect of your
relationship today?

■ What have been the happiest or most meaningful events in
your relationship, and why were they so pleasing to you?

5

Good parenting requires a purposeful commitment to values and character building.

CHAPTER 5

The Story in Their Eyes

If you bungle raising your children, I don't think whatever else you do well matters very much. *—Jacqueline Kennedy Onassis*

T he executives I advise have awesome responsibilities for their businesses. However, the well-integrated among them invariably have their children's ability to thrive, in every sense of the word, always on their minds. They constantly monitor their children's level of resiliency much in the same way they monitor the performance data that is projected onto the windshield of their high-tech automobiles.

Our children's lives are constantly in our faces.

It is not surprising then, that when these executives *get* the **Third Circle** concept, they invariably want my advice on how to help their children envision their own "Third Circles," develop their own strategies to reach them, leverage their strengths, and cope with the saboteurs that might derail their dreams. As the former First Lady so succinctly observed, if we bungle raising our children, what else matters?

No social institution, organization, or example of routine everyday interaction can survive without trust. It is the *sine qua non* of social life. Indeed, the social scientist Erik Erikson suggests that every stage of development that we negotiate through life begins with the challenge of trust (versus mistrust). In other words, trust is one of the very first lessons we learn as infants. The basic blocks of social life rest upon the establishment and the growth of trusting relationships.

Sadly, our children's lives often pass before us in an instant, or we only engage with them when there is a behavioral problem. Interestingly, there is growing evidence from evolutionary and developmental psychology that the healthy development of the self, or the ego, that is essential for emotional intelligence is set very early in life.

> Interestingly, there is growing evidence from evolutionary and developmental psychology that the healthy development of the self, or the ego, that is essential for emotional intelligence is set very early in life.

In fact, we enter the world "hardwired" to make social connections. We are born physically premature and are highly dependent on caregivers. We must become bonded to a primary caregiver early in life in order to flourish emotionally[1]. This attachment figure becomes part of a child's inner landscape. Our emotions are the basis for our intelligence, as well as our morality and self-esteem, because all of the mind's higher functions require affect or intent-and-affect-mediated generative thought.

There are critical stages in the mind's early growth that occur even before the first thoughts are registered. At each stage, certain critical experiences are necessary. These experiences are not cognitive; but instead they are types of subtle emotional exchanges.

The first stage in the development of the emotional architecture of the mind is making sense of sensation. The infant responds with attention, interest, and pleasure to sensations such as touch and sound provided by a familiar caregiver. It is only a matter of hours before an infant can actually mimic a caregiver's expressions. These emotions help babies organize their senses and motor responses and develop a sense of security. If the infant is deprived of touching and talking, or if the touching and talking are negative, the infant will respond with apathy and despondency. Moreover, if this is not achieved, several emotional problems can develop, including psychosis.

The second stage is when emotions go from simply organizers to relationship builders and social communicators. By four months, the baby is exhibiting organized joyful engaging and, by nine months, we can see two-way, affect-based communication. The caregiver and the child mutually fall in love, leading to the powerful intoxication of human closeness. We are witnessing the early forms of communication and thinking. In truth, we are social beings from the very start. We are born to engage with others. We are born to trust.

The third stage helps the child define what separates him or her from others. The child who is met with unresponsive caregivers at this stage fails to establish effective boundaries and recognize that others are separate emotional beings. All of this happens in the first year of life.

If the infant is deprived of touching and talking, or if the touching and talking are negative, the infant will respond with apathy and despondency.

By twelve to eighteen months, these emotional cues and responses become the building blocks of increasingly complicated problem-solving as the child figures out how the world works. Pointing at a toy and gesturing that he or she wants it is an example of early scientific thinking as well as the ability to negotiate social relationships.

In the fourth stage, infants connect sensation and emotion to intentional action. Next, affects are linked to symbols to give the symbols purpose and meaning, and we see pretend play or verbal expressions of wishes such as "I want some milk!" Finally, the child is able to combine his or her emotional ideas with someone else's. This forms the basis for symbolic meaning, including the ability to think. The ability to intuitively grasp the feelings and desires of another through the emotional signals they send is what makes possible reality testing and other forms of logical thinking.

How children experience these critical affective interactions depends on how their nervous systems respond to and process physical sensations. The child who is over-reactive to sensation experience may require extra protection and soothing, while the one who is under-sensitive to touch and sound may require energized, intense interactions. By understanding a child's individual differences and developmental level, we can help the child negotiate the emotional interactions that lead to emotional health and intelligence rather than apathy, self-absorption, impulsivity, concrete and disorganized thinking, and language and learning problems.

> Our sense of self, our intelligence, and the mental and social health of our nation, suffers when we miss any of the required steps of emotional experience.

Our sense of self, our intelligence, and the mental and social health of our nation suffers when we miss any of the required steps of emotional experience. By extension, the impact of emotional experience on violence, international understanding, and the practice of psychotherapy may be significant.

It doesn't take much of a leap to see the connection, thirty or forty years later, to the "First Circle" in a workplace or to an executive's ability to see, sell, and create a "Third Circle" for his or her enterprise or family.

In truth, children are continually moving through developmental stages. Some are more traumatic than others for both children and their parents. For example, the "terrible twos" is sometimes referred to as the first adolescence. Saint Francis Xavier extolled: "Give me the child until he or she is seven and anyone may have them afterward."

A child's individual destiny is assumed to be formed in three critical stages. The first is around nine years of age; the second around 11 years of age, when the limbs become lanky; and at puberty, up until 16 years when the true individual breaks through. Coincidentally, these stages often occur when important opportunities and demands present themselves in a parent's career. This can lead to troubling conflict within the parent/executive. This gives credibility to the Spanish proverb: "A rich child often sits in a poor mother's lap."

As a parent and an educator, and perhaps because of the influence of the United States space program of the 1960s and 1970s upon my generation, it has been my observation that, metaphorically speaking, children "go behind the moon" at about age ten and, essentially, are out of radio touch! When they return, they may leave home and be gone forever. It is scary to acknowledge that, as parents, we may have less than ten years during which we can set the emotional and relational trajectories of our children or to share with them what we stand for and model ways to cope with adversity.

> It doesn't take much of a leap to see the connection, thirty or forty years later, to the "First Circle" in a workplace or to an executive's ability to see, sell, and create a "Third Circle" for his or her enterprise or family.

CHALLENGES TO RAISING EMOTIONALLY HEALTHY CHILDREN

Our company, through its employee services division, has contracts with hundreds of corporations across North America as well as internationally. Our employee assistance program (EAP) is vital to the health of our client organizations. It helps workers and their household members manage issues that may adversely impact their work or their personal lives. EAP counselors typically provide assessment, support, and if needed, referral to additional resources.

The issues for which EAPs provide support vary, but examples include substance abuse; safe working environment; emotional distress; major life events, including births, accidents, and deaths; health care concerns; financial or legal concerns; family/personal relationship issues; work relationship issues; and concerns about aging parents.

By far the majority of issues we deal with pertain to family/personal relationships, and a significant number of these involve the challenges of raising emotionally healthy children. We see everything! But, despite the challenges families face today in raising emotionally healthy children, it is clear that children are no different today than they were years ago. However, family life is very different. Children's lives are more active; they are overscheduled, and typically the family does not eat together.

Our counselors observe that children who are labeled "troubled" tend to be negative and expect life to go badly. They are ineffective in making and keeping friends; they do not cope well with everyday problems; they cannot talk about their feelings; they are not strongly in love with one or both parents; they do not like themselves; and they are self-defeating—doing things that only make their lives worse.

> But, despite the challenges families face today in raising emotionally healthy children, it is clear that children are no different today than they were years ago. However, family life is very different.

Counseling often reveals that their parents may not have the skills to cope with their own emotions, let alone those of their children. They may love their children too much or have difficulty disciplining when needed. Wealth often heightens some risks. For example, many children of baby boomers grew into adolescence taking financial security for granted. Lavishing money and material goods on children can disrupt a child's healthy development, erode his or her work ethic, and skew his or her priorities. Moreover, these children may be spoiled, undisciplined, overindulged, overscheduled, or permitted to be unpleasant and irresponsible toward others. These children need to develop personal values.

Affluent parents must spend time with their children, provide appropriate discipline, and establish a life structure that reflects the practice of virtues. They should also work less and socialize more with their children. Good parenting requires a purposeful commitment to values and character building. In truth, it requires even more effort than building a career that produces financial wealth. "Children will not remember you for the material things you provided but for the feeling that you cherised them," wrote Richard L. Evans who is best known for his inspirational messages given in the long-running weekly radio program *Music and the Spoken Word* with the Mormon Tabernacle Choir.

Lastly, overprotection can deny children the learning and confidence building that comes from making mistakes. Children are not born with a fear of failure. Rather, they are born with loads of courage, persistence, positive attitude, and self-confidence. They learn their fears and phobias from their parents. Worse still are those parents who create problems for their children by belittling them in front of others, scolding them in public, treating them as objects rather than as people, preventing healthy risk taking, failing to compliment their children's achievements, or by lying to them. Remember Albert Einstein's caution: "Whoever is careless with the truth in small matters cannot be trusted with the important matters."

DEVELOPING SELF-CONFIDENCE IN CHILDREN

As a parent, there is nothing more satisfying than to watch your child see, pursue, and achieve his or her own "Third Circle." However, "If you must hold yourself up to your children as an object lesson," wrote George Bernard Shaw, "hold yourself up as a warning and not as an example." Put the oxygen mask on yourself first! It is our primary responsibility, as parents, to nurture the development of self-confidence in our children.

Self-confidence is the learned belief that we can handle a certain situation correctly, knowing that we do not lack any of the necessary skills in order

As a parent, there is nothing more satisfying than to watch your child see, pursue, and achieve his or her own "Third Circle."

to successfully complete a task. To be able to do this, children need to learn to trust the world and feel optimistic that most people will be good to them. They need to make and keep friends; communicate their feelings so others can understand their needs; love both parents and feel connected to them; like and feel special about themselves; and cope with life's problems without making things worse by relying on self-defeating solutions— hitting *The Wall* in the "Second Circle."

> Parents affect character and competency development by inducing the right amount of frustration within their child. It is through the resolution of this frustration that character is formed and ethical behavior is developed.

Parents affect character and competency development by inducing the right amount of frustration within their child. It is through the resolution of this frustration that character is formed and ethical behavior is developed. In the words of Franklin Delano Roosevelt, "We cannot always build the future for our youth, but we can build our youth for the future."

Children need the confidence and the tools to be able to make good decisions, to break down formidable tasks into smaller, workable tasks, to organize themselves, and to have the ability to overcome challenges and setbacks while leading a happy, productive life.

Confident children with high self-esteem have had the chance to try things and get frustrated and fail and be upset and be sad and then try again and get frustrated and try again and then succeed. This is the most important building block for self-confidence. But be aware: there are different confidence levels for different activities. For example, driving a car may have a different confidence level than public speaking. Also, confidence is not constant with time.

Our daughter, Moira, who is now the chief executive officer of our company, was acknowledged recently as one of the top twenty-five women leaders in our community. As part of the recognition, each of the recipients was asked to speak for fifteen seconds on what advice they would give themselves if they were eighteen years old again and knew what they knew now. Moira observed that she would have changed little for she was back in the city she grew up in, surrounded and supported by her family. But, looking out at the 600 people in attendance, she reflected that she would probably advise herself to take a public-speaking course in college!

> To a child, play is one of the most serious activities they undertake. Children naturally create "Third Circles" but sadly learn to compromise them all too soon.

Self-confidence is at the heart of a healthy personality. Try teaching your child new skills he or she never had before; be supportive when life hurts and disappoints your child; enjoy special time with your child at least a couple of times a week; reward your child when he or she does not quit; ask your child for ideas and opinions; communicate that mistakes are necessary and normal for learning to take place; and, most importantly, love your child physically with hugs, kisses, and touches.

Children need to dream, play, and experiment. To a child, play is one of the most serious activities they undertake. Children naturally create "Third Circles" but sadly learn to compromise them all too soon. Play is about interaction with others and does not require adult-provided toys. Children will decide for themselves what serves as a toy. Our seven- and four-year old grandsons love the remains of the 1980s He-Man toys that Mary Pat had the good sense to store away after our son, Seán, outgrew them. Play helps a child develop fine motor skills, logical thinking, and social skills. Real empowerment does not come from simulations. Actually doing it is essential to mastery.

Obviously, children respond well to toys, but avoid gender roles with toys. Also, be aware that video games tend to encourage passivity. Set limitations on television watching, video game use, and computer time.

Finally, I often ask participants in my seminars how they believe children learn to walk. Over the years I have heard all kinds of explanations. They put one foot in front of the other, or they fall down and get up again. Invariably, the answers offer mechanical explanations. I believe that infants, to be sure, get upright and are perhaps supporting themselves against something. But, at the moment they launch themselves, they see someone or something they desire. It may be a parent inviting them to come to them or to come and receive something. Regardless, they go out of balance, fall forward, but manage to find their footing. What they see at that moment is an infant's version of a "Third Circle."

DEVELOPING EMOTIONALLY HEALTHY CHILDREN

At times, children become stuck in their emotional development. As the professional counselors in my company do, help your child develop his or her own "Third Circle."

HOW WELL DO YOU KNOW YOUR CHILD?

How well do you know your children? Do you feel they know you?

> Can you be an "emotional coach" to your child, or are you the stoic and emotionally sterile, Victorian-like, father or mother.

William Shakespeare advised that "it is a wise father that knows his own child." Can you be an "emotional coach" to your child, or are you the stoic and emotionally sterile, Victorian-like, father or mother. Help your child become aware of his or her emotions; recognize an emotion as an opportunity for intimacy and teaching; listen empathetically; validate your child's feelings; help your child find words to label the emotion he or she is having; and set limits while exploring strategies to solve the particular problem.

It is hard not to project your own needs, desires, and goals onto your child. So what does wanting the best for your child mean? It may look very different from your own upbringing, your values, and your interests. Do you know your child's personality, abilities, and interests? Be prepared to let go of your highly detailed expectations for your child. Spend quality time with him or her in activities that reveal his or her true passions. Create an atmosphere of trust and acceptance and permit the experimentation that all young people need to pursue as they search for the right profession for them, the right life partners, and their unique roles in society. Adolescence is a tough enough time without the distraction of parental self-centeredness.

> Create an atmosphere of trust and acceptance and permit the experimentation that all young people need to pursue as they search for the right profession for them, the right life partners, and their unique roles in society.

Children seldom enjoy the same music as their parents, but there are subtler and deeper differences; for example, religious, cultural, and political beliefs, between you and your child. In some instances these differences extend to sexual preference. Your child may also value money, job security, creativity, independence, and altruism in very different ways from you. Stay calm as your child explores his or her place in the world and tests the boundaries. Most importantly, live your life, in all of its domains, in such a manner that when your child thinks of fairness, caring, and integrity, he or she will think of you.

RESPECT YOUR CHILD'S INDIVIDUALITY

Even before discussing the respect a child is entitled to, resolve to respect your partner's opinions. Relate to your child as a united front. Do not judge your child or humiliate him or her in public. Be attentive to your child's needs and avoid favoring one child over another. Only criticize when it is extremely important. Love your child and build his or her self-confidence.

Ease up on the pressure and allow them space. Use "please" and "thank you" with your children. Give your teenagers the freedom to choose the time and the location to do their homework.

Fred Rogers, the late host of *Mister Rogers' Neighborhood*, observed that "knowing that we can be loved exactly as we are gives us all the best opportunity for growing into the healthiest of people." Respect your child's right to be whatever he or she wishes to be. You do not always have to agree with the choice, but give him or her a break if the answer is "no" to the following questions: Is it illegal? Is it immoral? Is it going to make a difference in five years? Is it going to hurt your child or somebody else? Is it inappropriate for his or her age?

LISTEN TO YOUR CHILD'S DREAMS

Take time daily to listen to your child and express your love to him or her. Observe play but do not interfere. Similarly, learn what to ignore as you witness your child experimenting with his or her social interactions. Listen to what your child is really telling you. Is "I'm not interested in math" an expression of academic taste, or that he or she does not understand math, or that he or she wants your help?

> If we fail to listen to our children, they will eventually switch us off, and we will lose the critical intelligence we need to guide them toward healthy adulthood.

Listening requires time and effort on your part. I recall the lesson my wife, Mary Pat, modeled as we parented Moira and Seán. Regardless of the situation, she never spoke down to them. She assumed a calm voice, but equally important, she physically placed herself at their level, listening and speaking eye-to-eye with them. If we fail to listen to our children, they will eventually switch us off, and we will lose the critical intelligence we need to guide them toward healthy adulthood.

Also, do not worry that your children appear never to listen to you. Be assured that they are always watching you. Children have never been very good at listening to their parents, but they have never failed to imitate what they model.

COMMUNICATE TO YOUR CHILD WITH UNCONDITIONAL LOVE

As with leadership, communication is the currency of parenting. Words are very powerful, especially the words "I love you." When communicating with your child give plenty of eye contact. Failure to do so implies embarrassment and distrust or a sense of discomfort.

> As with leadership, communication is the currency of parenting.

Communicate with your child in a language that he or she understands. Show physical affection. As you read earlier, touch is crucial to healthy emotional development at all stages of life. Do not withhold praise and affection. Separate the child from his or her behavior. For example, we love our children for who they are, not for what they do. Unconditional love starts with a cognitive choice. Therefore, love with your head and trust that your heart will follow.

BUILD A HEALTHY RELATIONSHIP WITH YOUR CHILD

Establish and maintain a personal relationship with your child. Remember that you are a parent first, not a friend. In the words of Michael Levine, founder of one of the country's most prominent entertainment public relations firms, "Having children makes you no more a parent than having a piano makes you a pianist."

Pay attention to what you are modeling to your child by the way you parent. Who were your parenting role models? What values led to your own emotional well-being? Parenting is an ongoing stream of learning and teaching. It is about the initiation into the values we hold dear and to the behaviors we expect. Provide discipline and structure for your child. In fact, discipline is structure. Teach self-control and cooperation.

Provide clear understanding of what is expected of your child. If he or she only learns of a rule after he or she breaks it, he or she will become resentful. Provide good rewards for good actions but do not bribe. Use caution with punishments. Angry responses do not teach children how to positively solve problems. Instead, look at each difficulty as opportunity. Show respect for abilities, interests, and privacy within proper limits. This will help your child learn healthy boundaries.

> Parenting is an ongoing stream of learning and teaching. It is about the initiation into the values we hold dear and to the behaviors we expect.

Schedule date nights with your children as well as a weekly family night out. Weekly conversations with your child are also good ways to ensure that you are consistent in your relationship building. These activities help establish lasting traditions. Be aware of your child's unspoken assessment of your behavior, namely: "Don't tell me how much you love me until you show me how much you care!"

WHAT COULD SABOTAGE YOUR RELATIONSHIP WITH YOUR CHILD?

Sadly, children whose parents have divorced are increasingly the victims of abuse and neglect. They exhibit more health problems, as well as behavioral and emotional problems; are involved more frequently in crime and drug abuse; and have higher rates of suicide. Clearly, a healthy marriage is vital in creating an environment that can help children develop as fully as possible. "The most important thing a father can do for his children," extolled Theodore M. Hesburgh, the former president of The University of Notre Dame, "is to love their mother." The example we set, therefore, is potentially the greatest saboteur of our child's emotional health.

Remember, also, that we cannot teach discipline at a time of crisis. Set the rules before a discipline situation occurs. Children may need professional counseling if, for more than two months, their achievement in school becomes poor; friendships diminish; they become more unhappy than happy; cooperation with their peers becomes poor; you are feeling that it is not much fun to parent; or if family life seems to be dominated by the child who appears to be troubled.

It is important to be consistent at least 50 percent of the time. If you fail to do so, then you will constantly be in crisis control, with evenings or special events ruined. Teach children the rules, so that they know what to expect. As in the workplace, failure to comply with rules has consequences. Life also has limits. Discipline is often one of the hardest roles for a parent. But remember that parents do not need to be liked; rather they must teach limits and support the healthy development of the child.

> Clearly, a healthy marriage is vital in creating an environment that can help children develop as fully as possible.

Parents who over-react tend to create dependent children who cannot live alone or help themselves. Those who over worry create a child who is insecure and perceives a world that is not safe; everything to him or her is a threat. Parents who are always anxious and worried create a child who mimics their insecurities. The parent who lies to his or her child raises a child who distrusts everyone. When children perceive that they have been lied to by the most trusted person in their life, then no one else can be trustworthy.

If we do not take a child's opinion into consideration and instead make all the decisions for him or her, the child will have no self-confidence. When we call a child by names such as stupid or dumb, he or she will feel inferior. When we are constantly talking about spending less because we are poor, the child may develop financial insecurity and may do anything to earn money.

Dealing with teenagers can be particularly challenging for parents. Avoid the temptation to control a teenager or be overprotective. Be careful about

> If we do not take a child's opinion into consideration and instead make all the decisions for him or her, the child will have no self-confidence.

rules; instead just guide them. Unless there is risk of harm, chill out about their silliness, latest fashions, or weird haircuts. It is more important to teach them what is right and wrong and build their self-confidence.

Take care not to neglect the physical health of your child. Cook dinner and eat dinner each evening as a family. Serve nutritious, well-balanced meals. Enforce healthy eating habits and avoid eating in front of the television. Ensure that you and your child get fresh air and exercise, preferably exercising together. Provide predictable routines with adequate downtime including enough sleep.

DO YOU HAVE THE DISCIPLINE TO RAISE AN EMOTIONALLY HEALTHY CHILD?

So can you avoid bungling raising your children? Do you have the self-discipline and self-control to be available emotionally for another person, especially a child?

Reflective Questions

■ What have been the hardest or most challenging events for you as a parent? How did you cope with them?

■ What would your life with your children look like on its very best day?

■ How has the relationship with your child (ren) changed over the years? How has your career affected your interactions and overall bond?

Employees are forgiving, patient, relaxed, and more engaged when they believe their leader gets it!

CHAPTER 6

Being Worthy of Trust

It is a terrible thing to look over your shoulder when you are trying to lead—and find no one there. *—Franklin D. Roosevelt*

Research by evolutionary biologists and social psychologists into the phenomenon of trust reveals that human beings are naturally predisposed to trust. As we discussed in chapter 5, it is in our genes and our childhood learning, almost to a fault. While it makes sense from a survival-of-the-species perspective, at an individual level knowing whom to trust is often a challenge.

For example, oxytocin, a natural chemical found in our bodies, can boost our perception of the trustworthiness of another. We are more likely to trust people who are similar to us in some dimension. If someone even slightly touches us physically, we are more predisposed to cooperate with them. We are, therefore, naturally inclined to trust, but we may be at risk of exploitation by those who know how to manipulate the natural inclination to trust[1].

Given that people are naturally trusting, it is perplexing that trust is such a big issue in the workplace. Are executives working hard to *lose* the trust of their employees?

> Given that people are naturally trusting, it is perplexing that trust is such a big issue in the workplace. Are executives working hard to lose the trust of their employees?

It is my observation that employees are predisposed to enjoy working in a job where they feel they accomplish something everyday, they are safe and secure, they have steady employment, the reputation of the company is positive, there are opportunities for advancement, coworkers are competent and congenial, pay is fair, supervisors are human, hours are reasonable, benefits are meaningful, and working conditions are safe. When all of these are present, the employee will feel safe, trusting, and committed, and will probably be there when the leader looks over his or her shoulder.

HOW ARE YOU DOING AS A LEADER?

I initially engage with my corporate clients when they are experiencing some pain. I strive to help them understand the true causes of employee engagement. We know, for example, that healthy and profitable organizations seek to achieve outstanding customer satisfaction and the equivalent of sales growth. This presumes that they have, and deliver, quality products and services. Many businesses use some form of total quality management to reduce defects and ensure quality. Too often, however, these costly initiatives fail because the human factors to support the processes are weak.

I believe that quality is sustained when an organization embraces the diversity of its workforce and unleashes the creativity within. But that will not happen if the organization does not create an environment of adaptability and openness to change. In turn, that is unlikely to materialize if there is not a culture of employee safeness, good morale, and a commitment to quality. Ultimately, all of this depends on trusted and effective leadership. The fish stinks from the head!

TRUSTED AND EFFECTIVE LEADERSHIP

Incompetent leadership is said to be the most stressful aspect of the job for workers; conversely, competent leadership enhances group performance and employee effectiveness and reduces absenteeism and turnover. When a leader fails, it is most often *not* a lack of industry knowledge or expertise that leads to his or her demise; rather it is usually an incomplete knowing of oneself and others, a deficiency of respect and quality communication, and/or a paucity of meaningful relationships that erode the foundation for *true* success and profitability and organizational health.

As a leader, you must inherently understand the *soul* of your business, have a "Third Circle" for the future of the enterprise, and have the entitlement and followership necessary to be at the helm of transformation. Again, in the words of Theodore Hesburgh, "You can't blow an uncertain trumpet." More specifically, you must have the ability to make sound decisions in an environment of ambiguity and uncertainty; take the necessary business risks; avoid being insensitive and controlling; and be able to deal with difficult people issues. Added to this tall order is the fact that in the wake of accounting scandals, huge pay increases for executives, and unpredictable stock markets, you will have to work even harder to gain the trust of your employees.

> When a leader fails, it is most often not a lack of industry knowledge or expertise that leads to his or her demise; rather it is usually an incomplete knowing of oneself and others, a deficiency of respect and quality communication, and/or a paucity of meaningful relationships that erode the foundation for true success and profitability and organizational health.

EMPLOYEE SAFENESS, MORALE, AND COMMITMENT

A corporate culture embodying safeness, good morale, and commitment is the backbone of a productive, innovative, and motivated organization—even in times of distress. In fact, after the terrorists' attacks on 9/11, it was observed that companies with a strong corporate culture were more likely to experience an *increase* in employee productivity. In contrast, those with unstable corporate cultures experienced upheaval, layoffs, and lost revenue.

> A corporate culture embodying safeness, good morale, and commitment is the backbone of a productive, innovative, and motivated organization—even in times of distress.

As we saw in chapter 3, job satisfaction is on the decline. According to a recent Gallup poll, more than 70 percent of American employees are "disengaged," meaning that they have mentally checked out of their current jobs and are just waiting for the job market to heat up so that they can go to another one. Often the problem is not that they are being overworked, but rather that they are not learning and growing in the work that they do.

For this reason, people development is critical to keeping employees satisfied and motivated. An erroneous assumption is that individuals have fixed abilities and work should be assigned accordingly. This does not allow for them to stretch and grow. In giving the opportunity to grow and expand into tasks with greater responsibilities, individuals will be more invested in their work, and managers and supervisors will have fewer responsibilities to shoulder.

ADAPTABILITY AND OPENNESS TO CHANGE

Without the underlying ability to adapt and change, organizations will not remain competitive. Successful organizations may be tempted to hold on to processes that are working, following the thinking of "if it isn't broken, don't fix it." This is often because change can be difficult; but more and more organizations are recognizing that in today's marketplace, the main defense against obsolescence is not constancy, but rather flexibility and adaptability. That is, organizations must continue driving forward and reinventing their businesses even in times when the economy would suggest retrenchment.

Niccolò Machiavelli, in his day, observed, "There is nothing more difficult and dangerous, or more doubtful of success, than an attempt to introduce a new order of things in any state. For the innovator has for enemies all those who derived advantages from the old order of things while those who expect to be benefited by the new institutions will be but lukewarm defenders." Abandoning what has worked in the past

> Indeed, as a leader you must have, and be able to articulate, a "Third Circle" for the company so that every employee knows and shares this vision.

is not easy. It requires understanding technology and the marketplace in order to know when creating new processes is going to enhance efficiency and productivity. It is important to combat the natural fear of change by identifying organizational risks and facilitating the creation of a culture of change. In identifying future risks or challenges, the human response to resist dramatic change is offset.

The **Third Circle** concept illustrates why many transformation efforts produce only temporary change. Lasting change, in contrast, is the result of a clear "Third Circle." Indeed, as a leader you must have, and be able to articulate, a "Third Circle" for the company so that every employee knows and shares this vision. In order for this to occur, clear communication that flows both up and down the ranks is essential. This will allow associates at every level to understand the direction in which the organization is heading, as well as what role he or she will play in its future. "A leader," as Napoleon observed, "is a dealer in hope."

Additionally, an accurate assessment of the strengths and weaknesses of those within the organization and of the organization itself provides a plan of action that will coordinate the critical balance across people, processes, and technology. Customized trainings (when combined with executive coaching and the resources of an employee assistance program) help individuals at every level in the organization to find this balance and ensure that all are working toward the greater vision. An essential piece of this is recognizing the unique contributions that each individual makes to the organization.

DIVERSITY AND CREATIVITY

Today's employees encompass a wide range of cultural and ethnic backgrounds, speak different languages, practice diverse religions, may be from a single-parent household, or may have a same-sex partner.

Opportunely, a valuable factor for organizational effectiveness is heterogeneity. Heterogeneity is the extent to which diversity among group members involving issues such as personality, values, attitudes, abilities, skills, race, gender, decision-making, communication style, and beliefs is held as an important factor within the organizational makeup. This may, at first, be surprising, given the tendency to believe that the more alike we are, the more we will get along. On the contrary, groups composed of members having diverse, relevant abilities perform more effectively than groups composed of members having similar abilities. This is because heterogeneity promotes the opportunity for divergent opinions and attitudes, freedom of expression, and better decision-making by team members.

> On the contrary, groups composed of members having diverse, relevant abilities perform more effectively than groups composed of members having similar abilities.

When operating smoothly, diverse teams and workgroups outperform homogenous groups on problem solving and completing complex tasks. Differences in understandings, values, and ways of viewing the world, however, can also create intra-team conflict. For this reason, diversity must be carefully and competently managed. Poorly managed diversity can lead to inconsistency, communication problems, and a lack of social integration. The result is low job satisfaction, higher levels of absenteeism and turnover, and ultimately low productivity.

Six years ago, Norway mandated gender equity on corporate boards. In a recent study of the perceptions of board members who were in place prior to the mandate, every single person said that the boards were measurably improved with the addition of women[2]. Respondents noted that the change would never have happened unless it had been required.

> Creativity is fundamental for organizational health. In fact, creating and learning are consistently acknowledged as two of the cornerstones of business excellence and productivity.

Among their observations were: men tended to be a fraternity, serving on one another's boards and protecting each other; women were more independent, interested in getting the facts, more prepared, and asked many more questions; men tended to shoot from the hip; women were more interested in how the organization actually worked; women did not just want to see a PowerPoint presentation, but also wanted to know who the people were; women tended to view the organization as a living thing; women also wanted the whole story and to get to the underlying issue and continued to stay with that uncomfortable feeling that something was wrong until they found out what it was.

Since that time the governments of Belgium, France, and Italy have followed suit and set quotas for women on boards. The European Commission is considering imposing similar rules across the European Union.

Creativity is fundamental for organizational health. In fact, creating and learning are consistently acknowledged as two of the cornerstones of business excellence and productivity. Eric Hoffer, the philosopher and social psychologist, reminded us that "in times of change, learners inherit the Earth, while the learned find themselves beautifully equipped to deal with a world that no longer exists." Creativity cannot flourish in an environment where people are not permitted to fail—no one is going to stick out his or her neck if there is a fear that it might be cut off.

Creativity can be promoted within work groups through autonomy in the work that individuals do, encouragement and support of creativity, a mutual openness to ideas while also constructively challenging new ideas, and shared goals and commitments. Healthy organizations accomplish this by focusing on five key factors: organizational climate; leadership style; organizational culture; resources and skills; and the structure and systems of an organization[2].

QUALITY PRODUCTS AND SERVICES

A total quality initiative, such as the ubiquitous Six Sigma program, when supported by a focus on trusted and effective leadership, employee safeness, adaptability and openness to change, and diversity and creativity, can promote organizational health and ensure quality products and services. Given that the quality of products in general has improved significantly since the 1980s, a high quality product is no longer sufficient to claim a competitive advantage. Beyond the quality of the product, the consumer must feel a sense of personal attachment, or relationship, to the product.

> More and more organizations are recognizing that the company that cares about people, both the people who work there and the people who buy the products, will be successful in maintaining a loyal customer base.

CUSTOMER SATISFACTION AND SALES GROWTH

More and more organizations are recognizing that the company that cares about people, both the people who work there and the people who buy the products, will be successful in maintaining a loyal customer base. "Exceed the expectations of your employees," said Howard Schultz, the CEO and chairman of Starbucks, "if you want to exceed the expectations of the customer." But be authentic in your relationships with both employees and customers.

ARE YOU WORTHY OF TRUST?

In order for you to promote trust, you must understand how trust is experienced and understood by those with whom you work, as well as the feelings, beliefs, and meanings that underlie trust. Most of the interactions that occur within an organization require trust. This is because most of the interactions also entail uncertainty and, by extension, risk. Again, our natural inclination to trust and to be optimistic produces within us an illusion of personal invulnerability. Such is the challenge not only for the promotion of individual health but also for the promotion of organizational health.

Trust both requires and engenders knowing, respect, listening, communication, and relationships, and reciprocally, more trust.

Trust develops when successful behavioral interactions with someone are accompanied by positive moods and emotions. These effects create a feeling of trust and engender continuing positive exchanges and greater trust. When employees perceive the organization and its leaders to be competent, open, honest, concerned, and reliable while sharing values, goals, norms, and beliefs, the result is likely to be positive emotions and behavioral exchanges. These lead to favorable perceptions and judgments that the other party can be trusted and enhance the likelihood that the parties will develop shared interpretive schemes.

The distinctions in trust are dynamic rather than static and can shift from unconditional to conditional to even distrust when expectations are not met or negative mood and emotions dominate interactions. Therefore, it is essential that you continuously monitor the experience of trust within your organization.

As will be seen, developing trust among colleagues and subordinates is a reciprocal process. Trust both requires and engenders knowing, respect, listening, communication, and relationships, and reciprocally, more trust. Trust is set in motion with the exchange of information and the development of positive attitudes toward each other, or knowledge of self and others.

Remember—
every interaction,
communication,
message, signal, or
variance from the
expectations of a
relationship has
the potential to
diminish trust.

As we saw in the previous two chapters, trust is the number one contributor to the maintenance of human relationships. Once trust is established, individuals are more likely to give others the benefit of the doubt. Without trust, however, individuals may not have faith, even when the truth is told. Studies have shown that work groups characterized by trust make significantly better decisions, are more open with their feelings, experience greater clarity about group goals, search for more alternative solutions, have greater levels of mutual influence, and express more unity as a management team. Clearly, trust is essential to your success as a leader and the success of your organization. Trust, however, is not easily manifested.

Remember—every interaction, communication, message, signal, or variance from the expectations of a relationship has the potential to diminish trust.

BECOMING A TRUSTED AND EFFECTIVE LEADER

HOW DO YOU KNOW IF YOU ARE TRUSTED?

One way to assess how safe your employees feel is to examine your workplace patterns. For example, specific signs and symptoms of insecurity and stress in the workplace include excessive absenteeism, apathy, lack of teamwork, and poor motivation. These elements create staffing difficulties, decreased customer satisfaction, and decreased productivity and profitability.

Another valuable measure is your own commitment to involvement in the workplace. Besides leadership involvement, employee participation and work-group encouragement and support are significant contributors to a safe climate or culture. A safe culture can also be engendered by leaders who express consideration for subordinates; that is, viewing them as human beings with needs, giving accolades when deserved, and most importantly, displaying respect.

Leaders are attractors. Do you know what it is that attracts others to follow you? Do you know how others experience you? How do you dress? What is your leadership presence? How do you sound when you talk? Can your boss let you "out of the house"?

I sometimes feel that most of my coaching efforts with leaders are largely around this very topic. Take away your positional authority, and you may repel people. As a leader, you are like an actor on stage manipulating the emotions of your audience. Ideally, that manipulation is to heighten the sense of safeness followers feel regarding where you plan to take the organization and how. That safeness will, in part, derive from their knowing what you stand for.

Humans intuitively sense when others "get them." If you don't "get" your followers, you will lose your credibility as a leader due to an inability to steer others in the right direction. This is because an effective leader functions as a coach, guiding individuals toward their fullest potential. Essentially, great leaders, like great coaches, know their followers better than the followers know themselves. What is required, then, is a sophisticated understanding of people and their needs. Further, successful leaders appreciate that individuals are motivated by different factors, and they individualize their approach to members of the organization and the team, which allows them to get the best that employees have to offer.

> Leaders are attractors. Do you know what it is that attracts others to follow you? Do you know how others experience you?

Ascertaining your employees' expectations and discovering what drives and inspires them allows you to lead in a way that instills in them confidence that you will deliver, which will lead to safeness.

When I first visit clients, I am always scanning their professional "homes." What does their office reveal about them? How do they want to be known? Is it their diplomas? Is it what others have written about leading? Is it posters with inspirational clichés?

A friend's eye is a good mirror. One of the most powerful instruments we use in helping executives know how others know them is our **Paradigm-based 360-Degree Assessment**. It is natural for all of us to overestimate how much we are trusted. The 360-degree feedback is an excellent complement to traditional psychometric feedback to help leaders know how others experience them, especially on the foundational levels of our **Paradigm for Profitability**[©4].

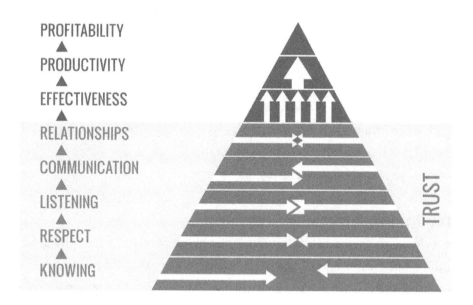

It identifies the *trust gap*, the discrepancy between self/other perceptions of trust. In truth, 360-feedback was created to help the executive appreciate the importance of the foundational levels of trust, especially among those leaders who thought it was solely about operational effectiveness.

The world revolves on the quality of *relationships*. This is the case in international diplomacy, business success, education, and domestic harmony. In turn, healthy relationships require *communication*—the currency of leadership. *Communication* presumes that we *listen* to the other person. *Listening* presumes that we *respect* the person to whom we are listening. *Respect* presumes that we, in fact, *know* the other person, ourselves, and how others experience our character, personality, and behavior.

This sequence—relationships, communication, listening, respect, and knowing—is *trust*. When relationships flounder and trust evaporates, we hear people say, "We didn't communicate," "He didn't listen to me," or "She didn't respect me." When we hear people say, "You don't even know me," we are in trouble.

When an executive boldly embraces the 360-degree feedback, he or she is signaling a concern about being trusted. In turn, the executive attracts the person who does not readily trust.

Highly successful partners in life, parents, public officials, diplomats, and business leaders have sophisticated insight into the power of the **Paradigm**. They understand what is meant by *profitability* at a particular time and place. They recognize that an error on any level of the **Paradigm** is enough to compromise trust and render the best of strategies impotent.

Our **Paradigm-based 360-Degree Assessment** instrument permits observers (such as bosses, peers, subordinates, customers, and even family members) to rate the executive on the various competencies we have identified *within* each level of the **Paradigm for Profitability**©. Collectively, these ratings yield a score as to how trusted and effective the executive is perceived to be. Additionally, our assessment center correlates the psychometric data with the 360-feedback scores to evaluate the challenge the executive will face should he or she attempt to improve his or her performance on a particular competency.

Remember: you cannot give what you don't have. For example, if someone who reports to you is expected to operate on the fly (a typical competency associated with sales and marketing) but psychometrically is an anal, rigid perfectionist who couldn't sell a pair of glasses to Elton John, you are trying to milk the bull!

> Remember: you cannot give what you don't have.

The specific competencies we measure relate to each level of the **Paradigm**. Such feedback, when combined with the insights from knowing your life's story, what you stand for, and what you do exceptionally well, can provide you with the self-confidence to truly *be* in your personal and professional relationships.

DO OTHERS FEEL RESPECTED BY YOU?

When you accept money from a company, purportedly to be leader, you give up the right to be ignorant about the impact you have on people. How well do you know how your employees feel? How safe do your employees feel with you as their leader?

By this I do not mean "touchy-feely" safeness. Rather, I mean the physical and psychic safeness people feel when they believe that their leader knows where the organization needs to go and knows how to get it there, at the same time respecting his or her followers' need to express their unique talents through their creativity and its expression in the work they do.

Within each of us is a desire to be creative, to be a part of bringing forth something new and unique—that is, to impart our unique essence. Each person's contribution to an enterprise is unique. As the late John O'Donohue, in his beautiful book *Anam Cara*[5] reminds us, work is where the *soul* of the person becomes visible, where each person's being is expressed in his or her doing. Therefore, in many respects, the workplace is a sacred place and an awesome responsibility for the leader.

ARE YOU LISTENING TO YOUR EMPLOYEES?

When you listen to your associates, their trust, motivation, and performance is enhanced. In chapters 4 and 5, we discussed listening as it applies to developing a trusted and effective relationship with your life partner or with your child. The principles are the same except that, in the workplace, you may be dealing with a highly diverse population.

Through listening, others are given the space to articulate their ideas and concerns, which allows their perspectives to be understood. Understanding listening preferences requires the listener to display cultural awareness, be sensitive to environmental cues, demonstrate behavioral flexibility, and rely on social composure. This is because there are cultural and ethnic differences in communication styles that play a large role in how effective one is at both listening and communicating. Given that today's workplace can be characterized as a multicultural, multiracial, and multilingual society, having cultural competence is an important ingredient for listening. To aid in cultural competence, distinctions in styles have been made based on culture. These are generalizations, however, and not true for all peoples of a given culture.

> Therefore, in many respects, the workplace is a sacred place and an awesome responsibility for the leader.

Individuals from Western cultures tend to exhibit "low context" listening. That is, they expect people to get to the point, assume that they do not have to rely on their surroundings for interpretation, believe that privacy is important, and take for granted that what is found in the verbal message is what is being communicated. For Westerners, the message itself is sufficient.

Those from Hispanic/Latino, Asian, Middle Eastern, or African cultures, on the other hand, may speak indirectly, be more circular, focus on the context, use indirect logic and indirect verbal negotiation, and focus on nonverbal nuances. For individuals from these cultures, the message itself is not sufficient; rather, these listeners rely on context (including previous decisions and the history of the people involved) in order to obtain meaning from messages. Knowing what to listen for and how to listen facilitates effective communication within the organization.

WHAT IS YOUR COMMUNICATION STYLE?

Motivation is important but not enough. In fact, if your leadership style consists mainly of motivational oratory, you may eventually run out of tricks. For motivational hype is like empty calories; there may be no nutrition for the soul. Communication is an extremely important competency of the leader, for it is the currency with which you purchase the loyalty and commitment of others. As a leader you are like an actor, constantly on stage, positively manipulating the emotions of your followers, explaining a situation, instilling hope, challenging your associates to deliver great performances, and exposing that which will destroy your "Third Circle."

> Communication is an extremely important competency of the leader, for it is the currency with which you purchase the loyalty and commitment of others.

Leaders are also salespeople. They are selling their "Third Circles" for their companies and the strategies that will ensure realization. Our studies of salespeople reveal that high performing salespeople feel entitled to the business they pursue and can ask for it. Selling is the only profession where you cannot blame another for your failure. It is highly dependent upon establishing trust with a prospect.

Remember that trust is like being healthy or well-dressed in that you do not notice it until it is abnormal or absent. When it is right, it is inconspicuous. For example, you notice the dandy, the tramp, the obsessive runner, or the self-destructive person. It is only when there is an error on the foundational levels to trust that the hand goes up alerting us about the absence of trust. This can take the form of a union telling a workforce that they can deliver the foundational levels of the **Paradigm** better than management can. Or it can take the form of employee disengagement. By the time the symptoms appear, the pathology may be well entrenched.

WHAT IS THE QUALITY OF YOUR RELATIONSHIPS?

One of the best examples of the power of the **Third Circle** concept emerged during our work with a 200-employee, $100-million plant in a major city in the southern United States. The plant had been acquired several years before by a leading supermarket chain and was part of its extensive manufacturing division. The plant was in a rundown part of town and occupied a square city block. The workforce was almost equally African-American, Caucasian, and Hispanic. Following a bitter unionizing attempt, which the company narrowly won, we were charged with understanding why the attempt had happened and with making sure it did not happen again.

Obviously there was a lot of anxiety among management when we arrived on the scene. Our solution was to apply our systematic approach to diagnosing the current situation, developing a "Third Circle" for the ideal leadership and work environment, developing the plan, and providing the support to realize that

> Remember that trust is like being healthy or well-dressed in that you do not notice it until it is abnormal or absent.

vision. The intended outcome was to create a community of which all employees would be proud, to keep the plant union-free, and to improve customer satisfaction.

In the beginning, anger and hostility defined the climate. One of the first things we did was to enroll the plant's general manager in my seminar "Trusted and Effective Leadership—Reclaiming the Creativity to Lead Change" at Ballynahinch Castle in the west of Ireland. There he met other executives dealing with similar challenges. Moreover, he developed a richer understanding of our philosophy and approach to organizational health. Trust developed between us, and he returned from the seminar serene, accessible, change-welcoming, and newly dedicated to involving others in the change process.

We administered our "Becoming a Trusted and Effective Leader" assessment protocol on the management team. It consisted of one-on-one interviews and psychometric testing designed to know the managers and, in turn, to help them truly know themselves and understand their hopes, fears, and opinions, as well as their strengths and weaknesses.

Typically, in these kinds of situations leadership tends to pathologize and blame the hourly employees. To counter this, and to reduce the debilitating stress within the plant, we customized our corporate health survey to prove that we knew, respected, and listened to the hourly employees. In addition to the survey, we held focus groups and interviewed every employee in the plant. We placed ourselves at eye-level with them. Taking the time to demonstrate respect and to actively listen to all concerned resulted in a clear diagnosis of the current situation and a much healthier dialogue among all parties.

I told the managers that they had completed an experiential MBA, because they had learned what it took to change the hearts and minds of their employees.

The employee corporate health survey showed that hourly people needed to believe that management knew them and understood their opinions, feelings, and issues of concern. This was demonstrated through meetings between management and hourly workers that were facilitated with precision by our consultants. Some hourly employees, who were identified as "unreachable" in the group meetings, were brought into the fold through one-on-one work. As a result of the "knowing" activities, the climate predictably changed from being angry and hostile to being relaxed and open, a critical pre-stage to change.

The management team was then brought together in a two-day, off-site retreat. The CEO's vision for the plant was confirmed by all—to remain union-free, to treat people respectfully, and to attain productivity and quality goals resulting in improved customer satisfaction. Aggregate results of all the "knowing" pieces were shared and discussed. A plan was created with six goals and their related strategies and tactics. Coping strategies for anticipated barriers to success were included in the plan.

Our consultants spent intense time in the first two months leading up to and including the off-site retreat. Implementation and support of the plan were accomplished through monthly site visits and ongoing telephone and electronic communications. The project finished on time, and all the goals were accomplished.

> Remember: employees are forgiving, patient, relaxed, and more engaged when they believe their boss *gets it*!

That plant went on to win the annual internal company-wide quality award four out of the next five years. Periodic employee satisfaction surveys revealed significant improvements in morale and a much calmer work environment. Employee stress ratings decreased. No one lost a job, the plant remained non-union, and customer satisfaction scores soared. I told the managers that they had completed an experiential MBA, because they had learned what it took to change the hearts and minds of their employees.

I also challenged the general manager to be extremely vigilant when hiring new staff, regardless of their level in the organization. First, discern whether the person is a giver or a taker. Second, do they respect the community the team created? And third, are they committed to personal and professional growth?

Remember: employees are forgiving, patient, relaxed, and more engaged when they believe their boss *gets it*! Does your organization have integrity, proportionality, and beauty?

WHAT COULD SABOTAGE YOUR TRUSTWORTHINESS?

Over the years I have observed three critical errors that managers and leaders commit when interacting with employees.

- First, they confuse intelligence and academic achievement. Just because someone did not obtain a university degree does not mean he or she is incapable of making astute observations that may profoundly impact the success of a business. Many of us have exceeded our parents' career achievements. I admonish my managerial clients to treat their associates with the respect they would have wanted their mother or father to have been afforded.

- Second, they fall into the trap of thinking that employees are not interested in quality. That is counter-intuitive. The brain strives for the pleasure that derives from executing work with quality, symmetry, and form.

- Third, they assume that people are not interested in being led. On the contrary, workers are desperate for trusted and effective leadership. They can tell the difference, however, between the true leader and the person who is scared stiff in his or her own skin. A human capital approach to management assumes that humans desire to participate fully, to realize their "higher needs" of autonomy and self-actualization, and to identify with the goals of the organization. They will do so if the leadership and structure of the organization will permit it.

> Remember too that building trust takes more than twice the time it takes to destroy it.

Remember that employees are forgiving, patient, relaxed, and more engaged when their boss gets the human factors. Lead by remembering what it was like to follow. This will inspire trust. Remember too that building trust takes more than twice the time it takes to destroy it. Increasingly, employees are becoming sensitized to detect the fake outward signs of trustworthiness.

The leader who displays the competencies related to the foundational levels of the **Paradigm** will engender trust and loyalty in his or her employees. Typically, when leaders fail to sustain trust:

- They fail to see the big picture and do not understand what truly causes *profitability*. They fail to see the crucial role that human factors play in the realization of profitability, focusing on the nuts and bolts (the *hardware* of productivity and profitability) while ignoring or downplaying human factors (the *software* that makes the hardware run). Moreover, leadership is about doing the right things; management is about doing things right.

- They cannot collaborate for *productivity*—an essential skill for executing the business plan. Modern organizations have to be organic in the sense that their survival and continual development demands relationships that are interdependent, collaborative, and characterized by trust. Paradoxically (given the importance of interdependence and collaboration), there has to be an organizational commitment to provide as much autonomy as it is possible to grant, limited only by the level at which employees are willing to accept it. Organizational and team unity allows businesses to attack problems as a collaborative unit. A divided company results in estranged relationships, corporate backstabbing, poor group ethos, and an inability to effectively handle change. On the other hand, it is well documented that unity through demonstration of respect, listening, communication, and relationship-building boosts safeness, morale, and commitment, and enhances worker performance. Feeling safe will also lead to adaptability, the true measure of personal and organizational health.

- They lack vitality and *effectiveness*, suffering instead from stress, anxiety, uncertainty, and guilt. These in turn are associated with a feeling of loss of control. Instead of the leaders taking charge of circumstances, circumstances are in control. Eleanor Roosevelt noted that "you gain strength, courage, and confidence by every experience in which you really stop to look fear in the face. You must do the thing you think you cannot do."

- They are destroyers of *relationships* instead of attracters of followers. They fail to nurture the human potential in their employees and corrosively undermine the avenue through which our social and psychological needs are met. There are basic human needs for affiliation. The need to belong is one of the most powerful human needs. This sense of belonging, of being attached, derives from people sharing a common set of cultural attributes. Culture, for the anthropologist or sociologist, has an explanatory power similar to that of gravity for the physicist. If there is not an official culture with values, attitudes, and so forth, that employees can identify with and buy into, then one will emerge to fill the void—for the good or ill of the corporation. Relationships bind us, one to the other, to organizations, institutions, and ultimately, to society itself. In turn, healthy relationships are predicated on knowing, respecting, listening to, and effectively communicating with others. People want not only to belong, to be liked, and to be respected, but also to contribute effectively and creatively to the accomplishment of worthwhile objectives.

- They cannot convincingly *communicate* their vision for the company. Either they simply cannot communicate or they lack the commitment necessary to realize the vision. As Peter F. Drucker, the legendary management consultant reminded us, "Unless commitment is made, there are only promises and hopes … but no plans."

- They do not *listen* to their customers, associates, collaborators, or employees. Listening is never a passive exercise. Listening involves the active *attention* to what is being said. The listener must *attend* to the speaker. Paraphrasing Winston Churchill, it takes courage to stand up and speak, as well as to sit down and listen.

- They do not embrace diversity—the evidence of *respect*—nor do they apply the golden rule, treating others as they would like to be treated, even for self-serving reasons. Leadership in this regard often comes down to the faithful exercise of human decency.

- They do not *know* themselves, their impact on others, or the people they lead. Without self-knowledge, how could it be hoped that they would know others or be able to empathize with them?

What *doors* do you open and close each day to make you worthy of the trust of your associates?

Reflective Questions

- What is your "Third Circle" for your enterprise? What kind of leader do you want to be tomorrow, in one year, in five years, by retirement?

- What have been the hardest or most challenging events for you as a leader, and how did you cope with them?

- What have been the happiest or most meaningful events for you as a leader, and why were they so pleasing to you?

Are you trusted to the extent that it would be unconscionable for a client to even think about leaving you for another?

CHAPTER 7

Honoring Their Loyalty

Profit and growth come from customers that can boast about your product or service—the loyal customer. *—W. Edwards Deming*

L oyalty is about faithfulness. It is also about devotion, caring, honesty, and even dependency on a product, a person, or a company.

At the outset of this book I referred to the security we feel when we enjoy the loyalty of our customers. Like friendship, the loyalty of our customers is a very delicate relationship that involves every sinew of the person and the organization. So how do you attract clients by the reputation of your commitment and by how you honor their loyalty? Sadly, we cannot teach someone how to authentically care. It is a product of everything we have discussed so far in this book.

Recently, I had an experience that goes right to the heart of customer loyalty. By any definition, I am a road warrior! Some years I fly as many as 200 times, almost always on US Airways. This story starts on the last day of April. I was flying from Charlotte, North Carolina, where I live, to the Ronald Reagan Washington National Airport. I was scheduled to teach a workshop the next day on my earlier book at the University of Maryland. Before departing from Charlotte, I visited the US Airways Club. I presented my card, and the receptionist politely pointed out that my card would expire that very day. I reached into my pocket for a credit card to renew on the spot.

"No! No!" she commanded. "Take this code and renew online tonight. You will receive two extra months." I thanked her and went on my way.

That evening, I had a dinner engagement with my client and did not go online. My workshop the next morning was well received, and I was in a good mood by the time I returned to Washington Reagan airport. I frequently work in Washington so automatically went into the US Airways Club. I approached the counter where there were three women ready to handle the afternoon rush. I presented my card to the woman in the center. She instantly informed me that my card was expired. Almost before she made her declaration, I also realized the situation and reached into my pocket and produced the piece of paper on which the receptionist in Charlotte had written the code to use if I renewed my membership online.

> So how do you attract clients by the reputation of your commitment and by how you honor their loyalty?

"I know," I said, "but may I go inside, go online, renew my membership, and bring confirmation back to you?"

She pondered my request for a moment, and I felt she would have consented had she been alone. Instead, her eyes flicked from side to side aware that she was being watched. To ease her dilemma, I reached into my pocket again and this time produced my Chairman Preferred Dividend Miles card on which it indicated that I was a one-million-mile flyer.

I continued, "Does this help? I am a one-million-mile flyer and have been for several years."

Her discomfort was palpable. She appeared trapped between two wardens. The woman to her left, who was busy at something other than checking people in, remarked, "All that means is that you've flown a lot of miles."

I was shocked by her response but kept my composure and, remembering the pitch woman on the Progressive Insurance advertisement, observed, "Oh, that's cold!"

Almost in an effort to break the momentary tension, the third woman suggested that the woman in the middle go back somewhere and request a fourth opinion. She did and then reappeared thirty seconds later and informed me that I could not go into the club but could go online there in the lobby.

If you are familiar with the US Airways Club at Washington Reagan, you will recall that there is a circular grouping of seats in the center of the lobby. I sat down and booted up my laptop. Almost instantly, my power went out, and there was no in-floor power source where I was seated. The only power was in the far wall across from the elevators, but there were no seats there. I had no option but to sit on the floor while other business men and women filed into the club and passed curious glances over my way as they enjoyed their membership privilege.

Every so often I looked up at the counter and wondered if the three women had any idea what they had done, how disempowered they were to make a simple decision that could have made a valued customer feel respected. Did they have any idea how unjust it felt or how words can hurt? Interestingly, I did not feel angry but could very easily have felt so had I not had a good day or if I had been stressed. Instead, I felt I was having an out-of-body experience watching a disaster in customer relations unfold.

Fairly soon, I noticed that the three women had been joined by an airport policeman who leaned against the end of the counter monitoring the situation. The message was clear. Instead of a valued customer, I was perceived as a potential trouble-maker.

Eventually, I secured a confirmation code, returned to the counter and presented it to the woman in the middle. She again consulted the colleague to her left, inquiring if my renewed membership would have already registered.

"No," she replied, "It takes several days, but he can go in now."

Before I left the club to board my flight back to Charlotte, I passed the office of the manager who had elected not to tell me in person that my years as a loyal customer were meaningless. One minute before midnight I was fawned over, while one minute after midnight I was a *persona non grata* in the eyes of that airline's representatives.

Clearly, American companies have much to learn about the foundational levels of the **Paradigm for Profitability**© if outstanding customer appreciation is to come naturally to all who interface with their customers. In the words of the American poet, Maya Angelou, "I've learned that people will forget what you said, people will forget what you did, but people will never forget how you made them feel."

As with other relationships, customer loyalty efforts can get bogged down in the "First Circle."

Most scholars distinguish between *rational* and *emotional* forms of customer loyalty. Perhaps there is also a more intimate or spiritual dimension that reflects how clients experience the character of a company. How are you and your company experienced by your customers on the foundational levels of the **Paradigm**? "I do not pray for success," wrote Mother Teresa of Calcutta, "I ask for faithfulness."

Are you trusted to the extent that it would be unconscionable for a client to even think about leaving you for another?

This chapter is also about customer satisfaction and how it begets loyalty. Customer satisfaction is defined as how products and services supplied by a company meet or surpass the customer's expectations. A customer is defined as anyone who receives that which is produced by an individual or an organization that has value. Customer satisfaction compares customer expectations to customer perceptions. It has become a key performance indicator and a critical metric of modern business strategy. The challenge for any company is to retain existing customers while attracting new ones, for the cost of finding new customers can be as much as ten times the cost of retaining existing ones.

Building loyal customers with service quality is a common competitive strategy for business success. Its effectiveness has the same ingredients that make for satisfaction in a career, a marriage, parenting, and leading. "Lack of loyalty," wrote author Napoleon Hill, who was the pioneer in identifying the power of personal beliefs and their role in personal success, "is one of the major causes of failure in every walk of life." As with other relationships, customer loyalty efforts can get bogged down in the "First Circle." They can easily fall into the trap of insincerity, superficial manipulation of the customer, or getting caught up in the processes and the quantification of encounters at prescribed customer touch points. Do you have a "Third Circle" to attract, develop, and retain loyal and faithful customers?

Do you have a "Third Circle" to attract, develop, and retain loyal and faithful customers?

As with our other relationships, we typically put a lot of effort into getting our relationships with customers started but tend not to nurture them and take them to extraordinary heights. Interestingly, each of the preceding relationships we have discussed has a role in preparing us for the demonstration of faithfulness and commitment to our customers.

Customer loyalty is so poignantly dependent upon the foundational levels of the **Paradigm**. Do you truly know your clients, and do they know you? Do they feel your respect? Do they feel listened to? Do you engage them in problem-solving conversations that yield mutually beneficial solutions? Do you enjoy the safeness that comes from an intimate, trusting relationship? How well do your daily actions demonstrate your commitment to your customers' happiness?

Are your customers bragging about you?

HOW DO YOUR CUSTOMERS EXPERIENCE YOU?

Despite all the surveying of customers and proselytizing about customer service, customers' actual experiences are far from satisfactory. Too often mature companies neglect the very thing that made them successful.

Too often mature companies neglect the very thing that made them successful.

Customers put a high value on polite treatment well ahead of investment performance and accuracy. Research reveals that 70 percent of customers leave a relationship because of rude or indifferent behavior by an employee. Interestingly, only 20 percent leave because of price or product quality. We want people to listen to us and to care about our concerns.

As with other relationships, it is scary to be involved with someone who does not make us feel safe or is incapable of solving our problems.

Disempowered employees drive customers away or miss a chance to build customer loyalty. Conversely, empowering employees to make decisions to the benefit of the customer and the company improves service quality. The truth is that if we are dissatisfied with a service we do not complain. Only 5 percent of us bother to complain, while 50 percent of us just go away. Forty-five percent may complain to front-line personnel, but they may not be action-oriented enough to correct our concerns.

Complaining to people who act like they know but do not care tends to ensure defections. The problem tends to be apathy rather than ignorance. Moreover, management tends to be ineffective and frustrated by company policies, procedures, and systems.

The breakdowns in customer satisfaction can be categorized into organizational, systems and procedures, or personal factors. Organizationally, we need alignment that allows employees to make decisions based on customer needs and organizational goals. As with my US Airways Club experience, the disempowered employee is strikingly obvious and speaks volumes to the customer about the values of the business.

Effective systems and procedures can help with such things as response time. For example, responding to a customer's complaint within twenty-four hours results in 96 percent customer retention. For each day of delay there is a 10 percent additional loss. The cost of fixing system problems is generally far outweighed by a high return on the investment in people. Similarly, teamwork and a linkage to interdepartmental objectives are critical. For example, a call to a salesperson about a billing discrepancy should be handled on the spot by the salesperson rather that shifted to the billing department at the risk of further exacerbating the customer's frustration.

Service quality is more than systems functioning correctly and employees doing what is expected. Service providers are the messengers between the customer and the company and vice versa. Most training tends to be focused on technical and professional competencies. However, customers like to interact with real people who do more than process and handle transactions. They expect good interpersonal and communication skills. Intuitively they know who is or is not working the **Paradigm**. They know who your top service performers are and will follow them if they leave your company.

> However, customers like to interact with real people who do more than process and handle transactions.

Do you understand the issues, costs, and impacts of poor customer service behaviors? Are you sending conflicting messages to your employees and your customers? Are you monitoring the changing expectations of your customers and modifying the delivery of your service and your product quality? Are you providing an outstanding experience?

DO YOU ENJOY CUSTOMER LOYALTY?

Human economics has evolved through several distinct historical phases, each one shorter and more compressed than the preceding one. In the beginning, it was the agrarian economy where people worked the land for their own food and sold or bartered the crops that exceeded their personal needs. This was replaced in the late eighteenth and early nineteenth century with the manufacturing economy represented by industry and machines rather than manual labor. With standardization, manufacturing organizations embarked on large-scale coordinated action. Interactions in the manufacturing economy, exemplified by the military, featured formal hierarchies, rigid roles, and highly controlled information. Horizontal interactions were discouraged.

Scientific progress through the twenieth century brought about the information economy. An early application and demonstration of the principles of the information economy was the infamous Manhattan Project that designed a weapon that used nuclear fission to create a level of explosive power that was previously unimaginable. Here the best scientific minds were assembled, and the burst of scientific thinking led to the realization that pooling information resources led to faster and higher-quality outcomes.

> They found that customer satisfaction had virtually no bearing on whether a customer returned to buy from a company again unless the customer was made to feel "totally satisfied."

In 1959, Peter Drucker coined the term "knowledge worker" to describe someone who works primarily with information[1]. Concurrently, W. Edwards Deming and others were inventing principles and methods to support organizational assessment, learning, and improvement and to connect customers, employees, and management primarily to eliminate waste and add value via shared knowledge.

With the elimination of layers of management and capital costs, the "virtual workforce" evolved. In 1990, Peter Senge's *The Fifth Discipline* proposed "learning organizations" to take companies into the twenty-first century[2]. With the rise of the Internet and sophisticated search engines, knowledge has gone from being *power* to being a *commodity*.

The way in which companies looked at customer loyalty took a significant leap in 1999 with the publication of *The Experience Economy* by B. Joseph Pine II and James H. Gilmore[3]. Their work transformed customer service and loyalty by asserting the importance of creating a vivid, memorable customer experience. The authors argued that companies could charge more for experiences than they could for goods or services. Customers, they argued, would willingly pay a premium for experiences that were distinctive, excellent, and memorable. "Memory" itself was seen as the product—the "experience."

To be sure, customer satisfaction is basically a psychological state. Thomas Jones and W. Earl Sasser studied thirty companies representing five different market sectors[4]. They found that customer satisfaction had virtually no bearing on whether a customer returned to buy from a company again unless the customer was made to feel "totally satisfied." Xerox Corporation found that customers were six times as likely to repurchase when they were "totally satisfied" compared to "merely satisfied." If a customer's experience is less than outstanding, it has essentially failed.

> When companies provide the ultimate transformative experience, they will be able to truly forecast customer loyalty.

Pine and Gilmore used as examples of the experience concept such companies as Walt Disney, AOL, Nordstrom, Starbucks, Saturn, and IBM. Starbucks, for example, does not sell the highest-rated coffee; rather it sells a one-of-a-kind experience. Pine and Gilmore predicted that experiences would eventually become the new norm and, in fact, commoditized. The final economic offering, they speculated, would be the creation of transformative events. We see examples of such transformative events in health spas and high-end grocery stores. When companies provide the ultimate transformative experience, they will be able to truly forecast customer loyalty. What experience are you offering? What experience could you provide? Is there anything memorable or positive (theatrical) about your product or service?

The Mayo Clinic took the experience concept to a very high level. For example, they required their physicians to wear suits when consulting with patients in a non-clinical setting. They even required all personnel to replace worn shoe laces. The late Song Airlines, a Delta subsidiary, took the experience concept so far that they forgot about the importance of the core functions required to run an airline.

Some argue that the "experience" concept is too top-down and makes employees part-time actors in the play. Might "experience" just be a fancy word for innovation? Is the idea of charging admission for experiences an out-of-date concept? Is the experience economy too company-centric? Clearly, such strategies may differentiate your company, but they only get you in the door. Quality still counts.

It is my firm's experience that most companies do not think about customer satisfaction in terms of a "Third Circle" and instead are prepared to accept the circling back and forth between the first and second circles as they receive data from the different customer touch points.

Lately, the experience economy concept has been elaborated by some into the interaction economy. This concept is based on the idea that well-designed, consistent, and regularly audited interactions lead to increased productivity. This strategy seeks to engender high rates of loyalty. It asserts that growing the customer segment of multi-level buyers is almost always more profitable than selling at top price. The goal is not to get the company to pay more for the experience, but to create value such that customers become loyal to the experience, as we see with Starbucks. Companies who foster the experience concept partner with their customers to maximize value.

In the interaction economy, collaboration is planned, controlled, and integrated into every touch point with the customer. Companies collaborate with their customers to co-create experiences, solve problems, and even design products. Customers are engaged through active listening in order to understand the customers' motivations, and the companies dig deep to explore the range of customers' expectations, needs, and aspirations. Every touch point is considered worthy of exploration. Companies search for the most accurate, bias-free information possible. Employees are important in the interaction economy and are thoroughly trained to test and measure at every customer touch point.

Despite the hype, outstanding experiences do not seem to have made their way into day-to-day reality in any notable way. The American Customer Satisfaction Index (ACSI) continues to fluctuate[5]. It is my firm's experience that most companies do not think about customer satisfaction in terms of a "Third Circle" and instead are prepared to accept the circling back and forth between the first and second circles as they receive data from the different customer touch points. They have vague plans and are inconsistent in their behavior. To be sure, when people are involved, variability is inevitable. Worse still is the assumption by boards of directors that management has execution covered.

> Start by showing your customer how good you are rather than telling them so. Such puffery will invariably back fire. Customers these days are very sophisticated, so demonstrate how much you truly care.

Do you have a plan for attracting, developing, and retaining loyal customers where superior service is second nature to everyone in your organization? Start by showing your customer how good you are rather than telling them so. Such puffery will invariably back fire. Customers these days are very sophisticated, so demonstrate how much you truly care.

You will not pull off an outstanding experience if you do not leverage each level of the **Paradigm** toward a faithfully motivated "Third Circle" for customer loyalty. The **Paradigm** is about *interaction*. More importantly, it is about the causation that creates the quality of interaction (knowing, respect, listening, communication, relationships) that permits effectiveness, productivity, and profitability. It systematically addresses the human factors that are typically

> As the demand
> for valuable
> interactions grows,
> the companies
> whose employees
> are most skilled at
> these interactions will
> have a considerable
> competitive
> advantage.

avoided or approached in such a fashion that the observed effect is just "doing stuff." No wonder that most companies fail to deliver on customer service.

As with most relationships, the ideal will come naturally if you do the right things, in the right sequence. As the demand for valuable interactions grows, the companies whose employees are most skilled at these interactions will have a considerable competitive advantage. The compelling customer experience is one that brands, sells, and inspires loyalty, even when customers may not be aware of exactly why the experience works. High-quality interactions do not merely coordinate action; they stimulate innovation. Continuous value innovation is the key to sustainable growth.

LEVERAGING THE PARADIGM TO BUILD CUSTOMER LOYALTY

The interaction economy requires three key competencies: clearly seeing a "Third Circle"; being able to diagnose and respond to interactive opportunities; and being able to work the **Paradigm**.

HOW WELL DO YOU KNOW YOUR CUSTOMER?

Most large companies use the American Customer Satisfaction Index (ACSI), a scientific standard of customer satisfaction, to help them monitor customer satisfaction. Research suggests that it is a strong predictor of gross domestic product (GDP) and an even stronger predictor of personal consumption expenditure (PCE). It is a *rational* measure that predicts customer loyalty, word-of-mouth recommendations, and purchasing behavior. It measures customer satisfaction annually for 200 companies in 43 industries and 10 economic sectors.

There are several other measures, such as The Kano Model, that classifies customer preferences into five categories: attractive, one-dimensional, must-be, indifferent, and reverse. J. D. Power and Associates is notable in the automotive industry. The T. Kearney's Customer Satisfaction Audit incorporates the Stages of Excellence framework. The International Customer Service Institute (TICSI) helps companies focus their attention on delivering excellence in the management of customer service while also providing recognition through a third-party registration scheme. Its Service Quality Model evaluates policies, processes, people, premises, product/services, and performance measurements. The assumption is that the implementation of a customer service standard leads to higher levels of customer satisfaction, which in turn leads to customer retention and loyalty.

Regardless of your size, it is important to build a survey that your customers have the time and inclination to respond to—one that delves into the types of information that will truly enhance your company's performance. Surveys are quick, cheap, and provide quantitative data and useful trend lines. They also provide the customer with the opportunity to vent. Sadly, too many surveys are an annoyance or are handled badly. Make them brief but strong. Be sure to measure from a variety of perspectives using a variety of methods to help confirm or deny the validity of your survey. Is your survey measuring the feelings and needs of real customers?

Unfortunately, surveys are subject to several types of bias: sampling bias, when the subpopulation being tested does not represent the fabric of the whole population; sampling error, where the sample is too small or non-representative; response bias, where responses may be skewed because of geographic, temporal (time of day), technology (cell phones versus land lines), motivation (highly satisfied) factors; or wording and execution biases, where there is a lack of options to select from or there is questionable wording, or there are bogus questions or happy questions. Responses can also be rigged when employees skew their own results, self-administer, cheat, or are pressured to get good results. Sometimes there is no meaningful information obtained.

Surveys can help you discover new product and service development ideas; determine what makes your customers loyal; understand customer issues and relationships to your employees; and achieve a competitive edge with satisfied customers.

Most companies these days also seek to benchmark against comparable organizations. Make sure you include companies that market a comparable experience to yours. For example, the American Automobile Association (AAA) found Domino's Pizza an interesting company against which to benchmark since they both promise to deliver a product or service (a pizza or a rescue vehicle) to a customer within so many minutes. Make sure you differentiate whether you are seeking a comparison on performance (quantitative), process (business procedures), or strategic (driving strategies) benchmarking criteria. Sometimes it is hard to standardize data when benchmarking, and the very activity may detract from a more evidence-based approach to management.

Benchmarking is also criticized for aiming too low and for not driving the organization toward the "extraordinary" experience. Typically, you can only tell if you are living up to the standard of another rather than breaking ahead of the pack. Stacking up does not confer a competitive edge! Another criticism is that benchmarking does not uncover root causes, exposing only superficial qualities. In truth, successful companies have both good and bad practices. Most important is to be strategic about what you take from elsewhere. Benchmarking does not identify growth opportunities or help you with innovation. As we noted earlier, continuous value innovation is the key to sustainable growth.

In contrast to *rational* satisfaction, which so many of the above approaches seek to measure, *emotional* satisfaction is evidenced by the feelings of confidence, pride, passion, and integrity customers exhibit for a company and its goods and services.

When it comes to customer loyalty, rationality is a myth. It is a fact that emotions drive customers' purchasing decisions, while rational considerations (price or convenience) are mere afterthoughts. Excessive surveying of customers and employees without responding to their emotional needs or concerns will induce the opposite effect to that which you intended. Customers may conclude that you do not *know* them or care to know them.

If you want loyal customers, develop loyal employees. Moreover, it is prudent, if not imperative, to retain those employees who interact well with your customers. These may be salespeople, technical support professionals, or customer-service people. Avoid just hiring or deploying the next available person to interact with your customers. We notice that exemplary performers manage roadblocks more effectively. They bend the rules and pay attention to the little things. The best of them are focused on doing the right thing for the customer and the business. They will make decisions, take appropriate risks, and take action. They have good self-esteem, are confident, and solve problems. Also, top performers think about past successes, while poor performers think about their failures. Can you visualize your "Third Circle"?

While information about *rational* satisfaction is certainly useful, your

> While information about rational satisfaction is certainly useful, your challenge is to match your rigor for the rational with a commensurate rigor for the emotional dimensions of customer satisfaction and loyalty.

challenge is to match your rigor for the *rational* with a commensurate rigor for the *emotional* dimensions of customer satisfaction and loyalty. Challenging as this may be, it will be truly transformational and distinguish you from those who approach customer satisfaction with a check list. In the words of Oscar Wilde, "Faithfulness is to the emotional life what consistency is to the life of the intellect—simply a confession of failures."

Reach out to your customers, not only to get a richer level of knowing them but also because the more contact you have with a customer the less likely they are to leave the relationship. The more your customer sees someone from your firm the better. Be known to them through newsletters, media clippings, free seminars, and so forth. Follow through on your commitments to your customers. This is no different than keeping your promises to your life partner or your children.

Allow yourself to emotionally connect with your customers. Find out about their lives, their hopes, their goals, and their desired outcomes for their businesses. Position yourself as a resource for life. The greater the level of connection you have with your customer, the greater the mutual satisfaction. Similarly, the more your customer knows about you and your accomplishments the better and, by extension, the greater trust they will have that there is someone out there who can help them. These interactions can take you far beyond the usual survey approaches.

DOES YOUR CUSTOMER FEEL RESPECTED BY YOUR COMPANY?

Do not equate customer loyalty with satisfaction. Many computer users are loyal to Microsoft but are not satisfied customers. I am loyal to US Airways but not satisfied. Customers defect because they can and because they are unhappy. Do you survey to ascertain a customer's likelihood of continuing to buy your product or service or to truly understand why they are unhappy with your product, service, or staff? The superficiality of

> Do not equate customer loyalty with satisfaction.

so many efforts is transparent. To reiterate the question posed by your life partner or child, are you truly in the relationship?

Complaints are your customers' gift to your business. As we noted earlier, most customers do not bother to complain, they just drift away. Be thankful when you receive a complaint. Do not be defensive; instead use it to build your business. The first emotion the customer is experiencing is lack of respect. As they further process their dissatisfaction, they may analyze it in terms of a lack of listening or poor communication; but the underlying risk factor that you need to acknowledge is their perceived lack of respect. Remember that you cannot tell someone how to feel. If you try, you will dig an even deeper hole for yourself.

> Complaints are your customers' gift to your business.

Complaints often stem from a customer not feeling understood or they feel like they are being treated like a number or a widget. Recall from my experience in the US Airways Club that one of the most hurtful emotions I felt was the lack of fairness and a sense of injustice. I was not valued despite many years as a loyal customer. At times like these, the customer does not need to hear "it is our policy." When those words are spoken, the customer hears employee disempowerment, laziness, apathy, or indifference. Instead, the employee should respond with empathy. In the US Airways Club, I never heard the word "sorry." What I heard was "got you!" Do not insult your best customer.

Emotions can run high when people's respect has been violated. Assume that the customer has the right to be angry or may even feel betrayed. Diffuse the emotion by remaining calm and admitting your mistake. Customers want to feel validated in their frustrations. No one likes to be ignored. Do not take the customer's emotion personally. Be polite no matter what. Say "please" and "thank you." Remember that you represent your company. Restate the customer's frustration and treat them like a real person. Resolve the issue quickly and in the best interests of the customer.

Do not send them on a wild goose chase like the earlier example with a billing question.

Remember that nothing gets accomplished by trying to maintain the appearance of perfection. Customers will only get more frustrated and angry. Be nice but firm and present with an attitude of courtesy and respect. When the dust settles, follow up with a phone call or mail a satisfaction questionnaire. Perhaps invite them to your offices for lunch. Strive for more interactions after the resolution of the problem with technical, service, or customer support. Support your employees through the process. They need to know you have their backs if you want them to demonstrate empowerment. Make a peace offering to the customer. This can take the form of a minor concession; for example, restaurants often offer a complimentary dessert to the customer who feels disrespected.

> Remember that nothing gets accomplished by trying to maintain the appearance of perfection.

Be consistent in your approach to and interaction with your customers. Be honest and deport yourself with a solid, professional style. If you hope to work your way up the **Paradigm**, your customers must feel that they can grow to depend on you. Loyal clients are the ones who believe they are receiving more compelling value doing business with you as opposed to your competition, and they wouldn't think of working with anyone else.

HOW WELL ARE YOU LISTENING TO YOUR CUSTOMER?

There is a saying: you may be looking but not seeing. There is a corollary: you may be listening but not hearing. If we only depend on *rational* methods to collect information about customer satisfaction, we are apt to be listening but not hearing. The main vehicles customers have to communicate their dissatisfaction with your company are complaints—if they bother to tell you.

A complaint is any measure of dissatisfaction with your product or service, even if it is unfair, untrue or painful to hear. Typically complaints are about: service, content, delivery, or quality; personnel; requests; communication; response time; documentation; billing; or follow-up. Customer complaints are like preventative medicine. They are the advanced warning that portends a problem in the relationship with your customer. Financial statements, in contrast, are historical data and of little relevance in understanding loyalty issues.

Today's business environment is fast-paced and complex. Those who represent your company must know your product or service thoroughly, have relevant company information at their fingertips, be comfortable with technology, communicate confidently and with savvy, and most importantly, listen.

> Customer complaints are like preventative medicine. They are the advanced warning that portends a problem in the relationship with your customer. Financial statements, in contrast, are historical data and of little relevance in understanding loyalty issues.

Listening is intelligence gathering. A small gap between customers' expectations and their perceptions can have huge repercussions on your business. There may be a flaw in your product. Your marketing material, advertising campaigns, and sales people may be inflating perceived value. To be sure, customers cause most of the problems they complain about; but when every sinew of your organization is synchronized, you may be able to leverage a problem into an opportunity for customer education and innovation. Listen for opportunities to train your employees, improve your products and services, and educate your customers about your commitment.

As we have seen, it is not sufficient to have the lowest price or the best technology. The problems with customer loyalty are largely related to the foundational levels of the **Paradigm**. Feelings of alienation set in when we feel we are not listened to. Like a lover or a child, we will disengage from those who do not listen to us or who listen with the obvious intention of advancing a pre-conceived agenda.

Typically, management only finds out about customer dissatisfaction when the customer tells them through voice (complaints) or by exiting (defections). The typical company response tends to be reactionary or firefighting that only further confirms the sense of abandonment the customer was feeling. Stop and listen to the voice of your customer and make appropriate improvements.

> Remember—when someone is asking the same question for the fifth time, it is no longer a request for information. It is a complaint!

Remember—when someone is asking the same question for the fifth time, it is no longer a request for information. It is a complaint! Solicit complaints and listen intently. Train everyone in your organization to collect and report complaints. Develop a funnel that channels complaint information into a central database. Organize the data into categories and analyze the data to see trends, patterns, concentrations, tendencies, and so on. Then use root-cause analysis to identify the source of the problem.

This may represent a cultural shift for your employees, so it is important to convert negative attitudes into positive ones. Keep your eye on your customer and identify an "owner" within your company who will be accountable for resolving the problem. Use the database information to improve your internal processes. For example, analyze complaints to define processes that are important from the customer's perspective and improve the most critical ones. Be preventative by looking for permanent improvements to such things as cycle time and complaint frequency.

Feelings, not thoughts, correlate with buying behaviors. Listen carefully to how anger is expressed so that you can make a root-cause analysis of the emotion. Listen to the emotion without emotion. Choose your attitude in advance. For example, declare ahead of time that it is going to be a great day! Visualize success, your "Third Circle." Demonstrate humor, energy, and enthusiasm. Resist negative influences and avoid negative people. Be a "whatever it takes person." Go around obstacles. Embrace change—expect it and accept it!

WHAT IS THE VALUE OF YOUR COMMUNICATION CAPITAL?

Earlier I mentioned that communication is the currency of leadership. Throughout this book I have illustrated how it is also the currency with which you purchase the trust, loyalty, and commitment of others—trusting relationships—whether they are with your life partner, children, employees, or indeed customers.

Currency, by definition, is a medium of value exchange that is backed up by capital. Your mastery of the **Paradigm** is the source of the capital behind the conversations you have with others. How strong is your personal human capital? As an organization, your human capital is more than your people. More precisely, it is your employees' mastery of the **Paradigm** to reach your company's "Third Circle." The **Paradigm** is often assumed to deal with the "soft" underbelly of business performance. To refer to the work of the **Paradigm** as "soft" is ignorant and naïve. It is extremely hard. But as President Woodrow Wilson observed, "Loyalty means nothing unless it has at its heart the absolute principle of self-sacrifice."

Just as complaints portend a problem with product performance or customer service, so too do angry customers who signal the company does not get it! As with employee attitudes, it is common to slip into the mindset that essentially pathologizes the customer or blames the victim. To be sure, the customer is invariably wrong or mistaken, but it is not prudent to tell them so directly.

> Your mastery of the **Paradigm** is the source of the capital behind the conversations you have with others. How strong is your personal human capital?

Handling angry customers is an unavoidable part of doing business. The majority of angry customers will continue to do business with you if you go the extra step to resolve their problems. This requires patience. Customer conversations come in waves; for example, they may be expressing sorrow or distress. Do not pour gasoline on a raging fire! Reiterate your compassion for the hurt your customer is feeling. Acknowledge their right to be angry and how the poor performance of your company was the catalyst for their emotional distress.

Speak softly if you encounter a loud and abrasive customer. Invoke a steady tone. Remember that the customer approached you for a resolution to a problem, so clearly they want your advice and help. They could have just drifted away. Confidently reiterate the priorities you feel are essential to resolving their problem. Be accountable and take ownership of the problem regardless of who created it.

> Communication in the thick of matters can get hijacked with the thoughtless use of email and voice mail.

Your customer does not know your company, your policies, or your procedures. They definitely cannot navigate the politics or idiosyncrasies of your business. Reassure them that you will be their advocate and that you will use all of your knowledge and expertise to make them happy. This is when you are selling yourself. Remember that outstanding salespeople feel entitled to the business and can ask for it. Do you feel entitled to take charge of the situation, direct matters, and reestablish the customer's original "Third Circle"? Place the customer first, the problem second. Triage the problem to understand what went wrong. Analyze the problem not only to correct the current situation but also to prevent it from reoccurring, hopefully not to the same customer.

Communication in the thick of matters can get hijacked with the thoughtless use of email and voice mail. When using voice mail, avoid phrases such as "I'm not at my desk right now," "your call is very important to me," "I'm sorry I missed your call," or "I'll call you back as soon as possible." Customers get very frustrated when they cannot get out of the voice mail loop. Tell them to hit zero. Return all calls and do not leave bad news on voice mail. Ask your customer for a call-back time.

The automated phone attendant is so often the first voice your frustrated customer hears, and it sets the tone for your business. Are you aware that you can change the initial salutation? Only 30 percent of calls are connected to those they need to talk with. Your customer wants to know where you are. Learn your extension numbers. Do not wing the message. "Have a nice day" may be perceived as insincere. Customers can sense your demeanor, so have a mirror on your desk so that you can be sure you are smiling when you pick up the phone. Every time you pick up the phone, you are like a radio actor in front of the microphone.

> Every time you pick up the phone, you are like a radio actor in front of the microphone.

The telephone is the only synchronous method of communication, meaning that there is a mutual back and forth conversationally. In contrast, email is asynchronous and dangerous since the etiquette is new. Be brief. Hurt feelings can sit for days. Voice mail is also asynchronous and, as we mentioned above, needs to be special. With snail mail you will have to wait for an answer. Fax machines have essentially been replaced by email. Face-to-face is the only form of communication that provides sight, sound, tone, facial expression, and body language. Maintain eye contact with your customer. Otherwise, you may look suspicious and be suspected of hiding something. Focus on your customer exclusively and give them your full attention.

When emailing, practice being clear and concise with your messages; reread and check spelling and grammar before sending; copy back salient points when replying to an earlier message; and use specific subject line descriptions. Since there is no getting your message back, practice the twenty-four-hour rule if you are upset. Avoid abbreviations and do not forward viral messages.

When confronted with a foreign accent, do not pretend to understand the person if you do not. Do not rush your customer or shout at them out of your own frustration. Never be rude. It is useful to keep a job aid at your disposal. This can include typical expressions, in the foreign language, that help you communicate your frustration or need for greater clarification. Regardless with whom you are communicating, avoid weak and wimpy words. Remember that we are all in sales, so be confident of your company's offerings and abilities.

Feedback cards are a ubiquitous and cheap feedback technique and allow your customers to communicate with you. Do you read them? How representative are they? Too often they are poorly designed and appear unprofessional. If they include irrelevant questions, they will only further frustrate your employees, your customers, and eventually you. Everything you use or send to a customer is a representation of your brand.

> Everything you use or send to a customer is a representation of your brand.

Interviewing is a critical strategy by which we communicate with our customers and probe the issues raised in customer satisfaction monitoring. When conducting deep-dive interviews with your customers, explore their perceptions rather than ask them to rate an experience. The interviews may be in person or over the phone. They may be with a prospective, current, or defecting customer. Your questioning may be either structured or free-wheeling. The latter requires highly skilled practitioners.

ARE YOU A PART OF YOUR CUSTOMER'S "THIRD CIRCLES"?

Have you earned the trust and loyalty of your customers? Are you an integral part of their "Third Circles"? Have you figured out what makes your customers faithful?

Relationships may involve different forms of faithfulness. For example, when the loyalty is of the low-involvement type, then the loyalty is habitual. All you need to do is encourage their habit. To do any more might be dangerous. High-involvement loyalty is rationally driven. For example, a loyal Volvo driver can articulate all the safety features of the car. When selling to such a customer, it is important to give them the reasons they need to justify their loyalty.

Emotional loyalty is seen with such upscale products as Burberry or Rolex, where self-image is important to the customer. Here it is important to keep the relationship alive. Some Volvo drivers invoke both rational (safety) and emotional (being a responsible parent) loyalty. When building customer loyalty, start with the rational criteria then ratchet up the emotional.

When your customer is frustrated and angry, they feel vulnerable and at risk. Through your actions, reduce their real and perceived risk. Communicate in such a way that they know what to expect. In chapter 4 I described marriage as a partnership. Think about customer loyalty as the natural consequence of a real partnership with your customer. Aspire to co-create products and services. People and customers will defend that which they have been part of creating.

Think about customer loyalty as the natural consequence of a real partnership with your customer.

Long-term customers, who are truly satisfied, are more likely to refer you to others and will probably purchase additional services from you. So develop a relationship that reflects a true service mentality. Demonstrate empathy without patronizing your customer. Do not tell them that you know how they feel or how they ought to feel. Do be enthusiastic and convey an eagerness to help. No partnership will survive if you do not accept responsibility for resolving a problem; it is your job, regardless of who was on point when the problem arose.

Likewise, take ownership. If you own a problem, you will handle it

> Focus your marketing on your existing clients. While some customers may be purely transactional, cultivate a deeper relationship with those that empower you.

better. Be resilient. Stay ahead of your customer and be the first to bounce back from adversity. Maintain your balance when your customer thinks they are always right; do not let on that you know they are not. Everything does not happen the way we want, so stay committed to your decisions but stay flexible in your approach. Ask for feedback and input. Create value, do the unexpected, and go the extra mile with grace and humility. Go deeper rather than wider.

Focus your marketing on your existing clients. While some customers may be purely transactional, cultivate a deeper relationship with those that empower you. Fully engaged and loyal customers, the Gallup organization reports, deliver a 23 percent premium over the average customer in terms of wallet, revenue, and relationship growth. Conversely, disengaged customers represent a 13 percent discount on the same measure. Reward your customers for staying with you, and leverage the loyalty you enjoy from your trusted and faithful customers.

WHAT WILL SABOTAGE THE LOYALTY OF YOUR CUSTOMERS?

Notwithstanding the importance of technology and operational excellence in ensuring a positive customer experience, how a company handles a problem defines the staff of the company. Moreover, it reflects its core values, its integrity, its own "Third Circle," and its capacity to make a commitment and be faithful. Does that sound familiar?

When customers observe that nobody greeted them; sales staff looked tired; no one said thank you; their phone call was treated like an annoyance; employees did not identify themselves; the person who answered the phone sounded aggressive and challenging; they were ignored when they walked into a workplace and employees continued talking and laughing among themselves; no management seemed to be around; there was no sympathy for their distress; and everybody looked angry—then your company has a problem!

Watch for team members who are having a bad day—their angst tends to carry over into customer conversations. Similarly, watch for employees who hang up on angry customers; do not return messages; put callers on hold without asking; put callers on speaker phone; eat, drink or chew while talking with a customer; interrupt existing calls to take others; don't use "please" or "thank you"; hold side conversations with friends; are incapable of offering more than one-word answers; use company or industry jargon; request that customers call them back; rush customers through their concerns; bellow into the phone; and not surprisingly, admit that they hate their jobs!

Such rudeness is an epidemic. It reflects a lack of the graces of a civilized society; poor education and knowledge, and a general ill-mannered and discourteous temperament. Sometimes rudeness is accidental and unintended; for example, forgetting to RSVP, perhaps because of being so focused, and ignoring others. It may be accidental but willful; for example, inappropriate cell phone use or sneezing into one's hand then offering to shake another's. It may be intentional but unintended; for example, not returning voice mails or leaving a mess for others to clean up. Lastly, it may be intentional and willful. Here we see the nasty, sarcastic humor or one-word answers. Such cold and uncaring behaviors are a customer satisfaction disaster waiting to happen. In all probability, there is also workplace conflict that will negatively impact your customer and your survival.

Organizationally, ensure that all your systems and procedures are working correctly; develop a compelling "Third Circle" along with an uncompromising commitment to your values; start every meeting with a positive story that depicts good customer service; make sure that everyone understands the impact of service on the profitability of the business; minimize roadblocks to action; have your team develop desired service quality standards; and reward good decision-making publicly.

If you expect to attract and retain loyal clients, then all of the above should be non-negotiable. It starts with you.

Reflective Questions

■ What have been your most challenging experiences with customers? How did you cope with them?

■ What education and training does your staff need for you to trust them to represent you to your customers?

■ Are you trusted to the extent that it would be unconscionable for your customers to even think about leaving you for another vendor?

I believe that, to a large

degree, we measure our

happiness by the quality

of the communities to

which we belong and that

embrace and support us.

CHAPTER 8

Standing Up

I don't know what your destiny will be, but one thing I know; the ones among you who will be really happy are those who have sought and found how to serve. —*Albert Schweitzer*

T he *doors* we open and close each day do decide the lives we live. Throughout my life, I have had the good fortune to have *doors* open for me or had the wisdom to close others. Those choices have permitted me to live in a variety of communities, as well as experience many more through my work.

I believe that, to a large degree, we measure happiness by the quality of the communities to which we belong and that embrace and support us. Sadly, the safeness we idealized half a century ago is so fragile today. I believe we have grossly underestimated the importance of community and neglected the creation of "Third Circles" for the communities within which we work, raise our families, play, and worship.

Recently, I had a poignant example of the choices one of my clients chose to make. The client in question is the chairman of a privately-held, multi-billion dollar industrial conglomerate headquartered in a major southern United States city. After discussing the various projects I was involved with throughout his organization I inquired what, from a business perspective, he was most concerned or frustrated about.

His concerns were less about his businesses, for they were well managed.

I was taken aback when he informed me that he was spending almost 75 percent of his time trying to help fix the problems with the public school system. My client was not just being socially responsible—adhering to society's rules and values—he was being socially progressive, consciously shaping societal values.

At first I was surprised, even though I know that chief executives spend a significant percentage of their time on community or governmental affairs. As the owner of his own corporation, my client was being intentional by taking a strategic and long-term perspective on the human capital needs of his business as well as on the quality of life in his community that is potentially at risk if there is a continued diminution of the educational level of future employees.

What is the quality of the community in which you live? Who are the real leaders in your community? What role do you play in serving your community?

For the past several years, I have been helping the *National League of Cities* in Washington, DC, whose charter is to support elected officials in the creation of healthy communities, reinvent its own "Third Circle." Because of that involvement, I have come to appreciate the incredible challenges communities face such as financial solvency, infrastructure integrity, clean energy, efficient transportation, world-class education, cost-effective health care, sustainability, and quality of life.

But creating healthy communities is our responsibility, not just the responsibility of elected officials. As Margaret Mead, the American cultural anthropologist reminds us, "Never doubt that a small group of thoughtful, committed citizens can change the world. Indeed, it is the only thing that ever has."

A PERSONAL PERSPECTIVE

Permit me to share with you some of the *doors* through which I have passed on my way to appreciating the importance of social cohesion—that which holds communities together.

I was born in the Glens of Antrim, an incredibly beautiful region in the northeast corner of Ireland. As a child, the first *door* was opened for me when my family moved to London. Most of my education, through my first degree, was in England. I lived in London during the 1950s and 1960s. Those were difficult decades in England. There were challenges as the country rebuilt after the Second World War. There were financial challenges, major labor unrest, and immigration that Britain had not prepared for, not to mention all the social changes that were sweeping the world in the mid 1960s.

On reflection, it was a depressing time. It was cold and damp. Transportation frequently came to a standstill because of the London smog. It was often quicker to get off the bus and walk than to sit there as it blindly crept along! I also recall how, as a child fresh off the boat, I would greet strangers on the street, as I had in Ireland, but receive no acknowledgement back! It was an early insight into the different levels of social integration and social cohesion that exist within different communities and cultures.

One of the first *doors* I chose was to leave London in January 1971 to pursue my graduate studies at Purdue University among the corn fields of northwest Indiana. I was struck by how unkempt the town was outside of the university confines. Despite London's challenges, I was used to watching streets be swept each day.

Following my time at Purdue, Mary Pat and I lived in St. Louis while I was on the faculty at Washington University. This was my first experience of living in a city with major urban blight. To this day, downtown St. Louis has not regained the social cohesion suggested in the 1944 movie *"Meet Me in St. Louis"* starring Judy Garland. Set in 1903 it focused on the 1904 World's Fair. In fact, Washington University overlooks Forrest Park, where the fair was held. Moreover, the university's athletic track, Francis Field, was one-third of a mile around when I was there. It was left over from the 1904 Summer Olympic Games that were held on the campus grounds.

While on the faculty at Washington University, another *door* presented itself. I was asked to consult to a hybrid seed corn company, headquartered in a small town in northwest Indiana. It was owned by two young entrepreneurial brothers. Following the consulting assignment, they asked me to join their company and lead the creation of both a healthy company and a healthy town. Initially, I was reluctant to leave the academic world for which I had been prepared but saw the opportunity to create an even more intellectually appealing "Third Circle" for my own career. I developed the company's human resources function from scratch, taught back at Purdue University, and founded a rural institute of preventive medicine.

This was my first experience with the interdependence of company and town. The owners' investment was a reflection of their values and their commitment to the community in which they were the largest employer. Unfortunately, that initiative coincided with the former Soviet Union's invasion of Afghanistan, President Carter's boycott of the 1980 Summer Olympic Games, and the United States' withholding of grain from the Soviet Union. That, in turn, resulted in the creation of a payment-in-kind program that compensated American farmers for *not* growing corn.

President Carter's decision changed the direction of my career and presented yet another *door* opening up to me. That *door* liberated me to formulate my views on the nature of healthy organizations and communities. It resulted in us moving from rural Indiana to Charlotte, North Carolina, the flagship city of the New South where I founded an institute for health promotion as part of the major medical center. After four years, and realizing that the hospital wanted me to make corporations part of its "Third Circle," I closed a *door* and opened another by starting my own company.

SOCIAL COHESION

For over twenty-seven years, my company's "Third Circle" has included the staff's commitment to support the human capital needs of our clients across the whole bandwidth of the human factors spectrum. In large measure, our efforts seek to create the social cohesion essential for human engagement.

Recently, I witnessed an excellent elucidation of the importance of social cohesion during a television interview of Gillian Tett, the British author and award-winning journalist and US managing editor at the *Financial Times*. She was asked about the financial prospects for the PIGS (Portugal, Ireland, Greece, and Spain). By way of background, Tett predicted the financial crisis in 2006. Her 2009 book, *Fool's Gold: How Unrestrained Greed Corrupted a Dream, Shattered Global Markets and Unleashed a Catastrophe*[1], was widely reviewed throughout the English-speaking world and won the Spear's Book Award for the financial book of 2009.

Gillian Tett's doctoral training was in social anthropology. Not surprisingly, she argues that the behaviors that got the PIGS into the financial crisis will not be the strategies that get them out of it. She asserts that the future belongs to the cultural anthropologists and sociologists rather than to the rocket scientists. She believes that the nations that most effectively manage through the crisis will be the ones with the highest level of "social cohesion."

> In large measure, our efforts seek to create the social cohesion essential for human engagement.

Social cohesion refers to the bonds or "glue" that bring people together. Dr. Tett, in her very British accent, remarked that half of her family is from the west of Ireland (a region where Mary Pat and I have a second home and with which we are very familiar) and that she had just returned from a visit there. She used the west of Ireland as an example of positive social cohesion in contrast, for example, to Greece.

In many respects, the phenomena she observed relates to shared experiences and values, traditions, family bonds, relationships within communities, peace and security, and trust. It also relates to friendships: recall the special relationship between the characters Jackie O'Shea and Michael O'Sullivan in the 1998 film *Waking Ned Devine*, which was set in the west of Ireland.

Family and kinship are the perfect expressions of what the German sociologist Ferdinand Tönnies called *Gemeinschaft* as opposed to *Gesellschaft*[2]. The latter refers to a group in which the individuals who make up the group are motivated to take part in the group purely by self-interest. *Gesellschaft* relates to associations such as the American Psychological Association, in my case, whereas *Gemeinschaft* refers to the intimacy Gillian Tett observed in the west of Ireland and that I experienced as a child and seek today as part of my own personal "Third Circle."

To be sure, *Gemeinschaft* and *Gesellschaft* are theoretical polarities. With the advent of the Internet, the concept of community has less geographical limitation as people can now gather virtually in an online community. This capability is having a profound impact on how traditional associations, such as political parties, trade groups, and knowledge workers, chose to convene.

> Regardless of your personal proficiency on the preceding relationships, eventually you will also be required to make choices about the relationship between your enterprise and its host community.

Throughout this book, I have argued that there are critical competencies you must master if you hope to enjoy a rich and fulfilling career and lead your enterprise to its "Third Circle." These include the requisite business competencies together with the personal character required to be a trusted and effective professional, life partner, parent, leader, and vendor. Not only are the competencies similar among each of these domains, but the historical evolution to what we consider morally acceptable, and likely to yield outstanding performance, is also strikingly similar. *True* success and profitability is truly a multivariate challenge!

Regardless of your personal proficiency on the preceding relationships, eventually you will also be required to make choices about the relationship between your enterprise and its host community. This is not to infer moral judgments about what you ought to do. Rather it is to acknowledge the realities about the interdependence a business has with its host community.

THE MOST ALTRUISTIC RELATIONSHIP

In the prologue, I noted that the relationships we have with our professions are somewhat selfish and all about us. The relationships with our life partners are a little more altruistic. The relationships we have with our children are even more altruistic. We are paid to be leaders and serve our customers. But the relationships we have with our communities are the most altruistic of all and reflect our mastery of the other five.

Altruism is the principle or practice of concern for the welfare of others. It is a traditional virtue in many cultures and a core aspect of most religious traditions. Altruism is the opposite of selfishness and egoism, and as Albert Schweitzer asserted, those of us who "will be really happy are those of us who have sought and found how to serve."

> But the relationships we have with our communities are the most altruistic of all and reflect our mastery of the other five.

The term altruism was originally coined in the nineteenth century by the founder of sociology and the philosophy of science, Auguste Comte. In simple terms, altruism is caring about the welfare of other people and acting to help them. Research has found that people are more altruistic to kin than to non-kin, to friends than to strangers, to those who are attractive than to those who are not, and to non-competitors than to competitors. Altruism is often demonstrated through prosocial behaviors such as helping, comforting, sharing, cooperating, philanthropy, and community service. Psychologists who study the effects of volunteerism (as a form of altruism) on happiness and health repeatedly find a connection between volunteerism and current and future health and well-being.

DEMOCRATIC CAPITALISM

To be sure, we exist in a dynamic complex of economic, political, moral-cultural, ideological, and institutional forces—democratic capitalism—that has evolved over centuries from such disciplines as philosophy, economics, law, history, political science, and sociology. Democratic capitalism is an amalgam of three systems: an economy based predominantly on free markets and economic incentives; a democratic polity; and a classical-liberal moral-cultural system that encourages pluralism.

The free market creates an intricate mix of supply and demand relationships and fosters economic growth, social mobility, and innovation. Political liberty allows for a constitutional system of government in which both individuals and groups are represented. The moral-cultural sphere, which includes values such as a work ethic, individual initiative, honesty, and respect for private property, is supported by mediating institutions such as family, church, and numerous other voluntary associations.

> The public's perception of fairness is critical to sustaining social cohesion.

Under the democratic capitalism system, we are free to form corporations as well as other types of organizations. The primary role of a corporation is the production and/or delivery of goods and services. In turn, corporations create the nation's wealth through payment of salaries and wages, purchases from suppliers, and financial rewards to shareholders. It is assumed that there is fairness in the distribution of the fruits of the enterprise among the various constituencies. The public's perception of fairness is critical to sustaining social cohesion.

To be sure, a business's long-term success is dependent upon the health of the society in which it operates; therefore, it is imperative that it conduct its affairs with respect for its impact on society and the environment. No individual, firm or industry is permitted to put the nation's economy at risk. The public good transcends the rights of individuals. In fact, democratic capitalism is based upon a balance of the rights of society with sufficient freedom for market capitalism to flourish.

CORPORATE SOCIAL RESPONSIBILITY

Social responsibility became a dominant topic in the early twentieth century when corporations were routinely criticized for being too large, too powerful, antisocial, and engaging in anti-competitive practices. In response to these concerns, some business leaders began to use their private wealth and power for community and social improvement. Managers were urged to be better stewards and to view themselves as trustees of a larger public interest. Accordingly, they were encouraged to act in the interest of all those who were affected by the firm's actions, not just stockholders and directors, but employees, customers, suppliers, communities, and society in general.

Which side of the social responsibility debate one takes depends on whether one has a world view that is characterized by *individualism* or by *communitarianism*. *Individualism* sees management accountable for the sole task of employing the stockholder's capital in the most profitable manner for the stockholder's benefit. This mindset is epitomized by Milton Friedman's much vilified maxim: "There is one and only one social responsibility of business—to use its resources and engage in activities designed to increase its profits so long as it stays within the rules of the game."

Friedman was an American economist, statistician, and author who taught at the University of Chicago for more than three decades. He was a recipient of the Nobel Memorial Prize in Economic Sciences and is known for his research on consumption analysis, monetary history and theory, and the complexity of stabilization policy. As a leader of the Chicago school of

> While managers have direct obligations to stockholders and employees, they should also address the needs of their customers, suppliers, creditors, and the larger community from which the corporation is said to derive its existence.

economics, he influenced the research agenda of the economics profession. A survey of economists ranked Friedman as the second most popular economist of the twentieth century, behind John Maynard Keynes. The *Economist* described him as "the most influential economist of the second half of the 20th century … possibly of all of it."

In contrast, *communitarianism* sees individuals as having certain social responsibilities to the larger community by virtue of their membership in that community. Here the corporation holds a social contract with society. While managers have direct obligations to stockholders and employees, they should also address the needs of their customers, suppliers, creditors, and the larger community from which the corporation is said to derive its existence.

Communitarianism as a group of related but distinct philosophies (or ideologies) began in the late twentieth century, opposing classical liberalism and capitalism while advocating phenomena such as civil society. Not necessarily hostile to social liberalism, communitarianism rather has a different emphasis, shifting the focus of interest toward communities and societies and away from the individual. The question of priority, whether for the individual or community, must be determined in dealing with pressing ethical questions about a variety of social issues, such as health care, abortion, multiculturalism, and hate speech.

At the turn of the nineteenth century, corporate entities felt little need to be responsible citizens. By mid-century, a few visionary companies, such as Johnson & Johnson and Merck & Co. Inc., identified corporate social responsibility as an explicit corporate objective. By the late twentieth century, stakeholder responsibility was widely sought and taught in most MBA programs, even if ethics courses were optional.

In truth, most of what is passed off as corporate social responsibility is largely a public relations effort. While in 1980 the overriding goal of management was to hand the company on to the next generation in good shape, twenty years later the prevailing motive was "build to flip."

The responsibility of today's chief executives is to manage the human, financial, and physical resources of a business to increase the wealth of shareholders, employees, and the larger community without compromising the world's resources

> In truth, most of what is passed off as corporate social responsibility is largely a public relations effort.

or the environment for future generations. The chief executive should lead his or her organization to be the best in his or her industry, not necessarily the largest, and to be the leader in quality products and services, operations, and people. It is not about building his or her personal wealth. Together with his or her board, he or she should conduct the company's affairs in a reputable and responsible manner, as defined by the culture in which he or she lives and works.

The truth is that if corporations do not get involved in the healthy evolution of their communities who will? As Andrew Carnegie, the Scottish-American industrialist who led the enormous expansion of the American steel industry in the late nineteenth century and one of the most important philanthropists of his era asserted, "Surplus wealth is a sacred trust which its possessor is bound to administer in his lifetime for the good of the community." Corporations are constantly required to earn the public's trust.

WHAT IS THE HEALTH OF YOUR COMMUNITY?

The recent economic crisis has had a profound impact, not only on careers and family relationships, but also on the traditional safety-net that community membership used to guarantee. Ironically, a statistical threshold has recently been crossed; that is, more than half of the world's population now lives in cites. These cities are highly complex and struggle to replicate the support that agrarian communities used to provide. In truth, there are communities within communities and "Third Circles" within "Third Circles."

Regardless of the scale or complexity of the community you call home, the communities that flourish and whose citizens are the most happy are the ones that enjoy reliable and useful services; are on the cutting-edge of innovation; are constantly renewing themselves; are safe; and most importantly, are led by trusted and effective leaders. Another useful diagnostic framework is to analyze your community's "First Circle" in terms of its genetics (governance, structure, and legacy issues); culture (values, traditions, and symbolic structures); lifestyle (leadership, collaboration, and followership); and access to care (professional support).

DOES YOUR COMMUNITY ENJOY TRUSTED AND EFFECTIVE LEADERSHIP?

Communities typically have two groups of formal leaders. The first group is the elected officials, who may have won their elections by their talent for articulating "Third Circles" for the community and by working the **Paradigm** to win the trust of a larger portion of those who voted. Like winning the affection of a mate versus sustaining a marriage, the talent for getting elected may not be the talent for running the business of a community. The second group is the professionals in city, county, state, and federal government. They generally stay around, while elected officials come and go. But they have one of the most stressful jobs imaginable!

While those who seek elected office are to be applauded for their service—for it can be a thankless job—sadly, history has proven that the motivation

> Like winning the affection of a mate versus sustaining a marriage, the talent for getting elected may not be the talent for running the business of a community.

for civic leadership is too often based on short-sightedness, greed, graft, oppression, and the pursuit of power. Globally, corruption is both a major cause of and a result of poverty. It occurs at all levels of society, including local and national governments, civil society, judiciary functions, large and small businesses, the military, and other services. Corruption disproportionately affects the poor in both rich and poor nations. All elements of society are affected in some way since corruption undermines political development, democracy, economic development, the environment, and people's health. While working with young leaders in Malawi, I observed how posters, throughout the country, implored its citizens to report corruption.

> Globally, corruption is both a major cause of and a result of poverty.

The informal leaders in a community are those with the energy and influence to work overtly or behind the scenes on important initiatives for the growth of the community or for equity and social justice. In healthy communities, these include the executive I mentioned earlier who was working on the public school system, as well as those who have particular talent around the quality, scope, and scale of the important systems that underpin the successful functioning of a community; for example, talented people investing their creativity, strategic planning, and capital resources in infra-structure systems such as transportation, education, public safety, health care, energy, and so forth.

An unintended consequence of the growth of the Internet, however, is the decline in the viability of local newspapers and, as a knock-on effect, the loss of investigative reporting that historically uncovered graft and corruption. Even with this loss, there is an epidemic of convictions of elected officials throughout the United States and Europe.

How trustworthy are the leaders of your community? Have you ever thought of running for elected office? If so, what prevented you?

DO CITIZENS FEEL SAFE, HAPPY
AND COMMITTED TO YOUR COMMUNITY?

When a community is healthy, there is also freedom and security. Community then takes on a life of its own as people become free enough to share and secure enough to get along. That sense of connectedness—and the formation of social networks—comprise what has become known as social capital.

> That sense of connectedness— and the formation of social networks— comprise what has become known as social capital.

Robert D. Putnam defined social capital as "the collective value of all social networks and species (who people know) and the inclinations that arise from these works to do things for each other (norms of reciprocity)."

Social capital in action can be seen in all sorts of groups, including neighbors keeping an eye on each other's homes. Putnam noted in his 2000 classic work *Bowling Alone: The Collapse and Revival of American Community*[3] that social capital has been falling in the United States since 1950. He used bowling in leagues as a surrogate measure for a disintegration in society.

For instance, he found that over the previous twenty-five years there was a reduction in all forms of in-person social intercourse upon which Americans used to found, educate, and enrich the fabric of their social lives and that this reduction potentially undermines the active civil engagement that a strong democracy requires of its citizens. He measured the disengagement from political involvement, as well as a growing distrust of government.

In addition, he calculated that attendance at club meetings had fallen by 58 percent, family dinners were down 33 percent, and having friends visit had fallen by 45 percent. The same patterns were also evident in many other western countries. Western cultures are thought to be losing the spirit of community that once was found in institutions, including churches and community centers. Putnam blamed technology for this decline in social cohesiveness.

The sociologist, Ray Oldenburg noted in his book *The Great Good Place*[4] that people need three places: the home, the office, and the community hangout or gathering place. With this philosophy in mind, many grassroots efforts, such as the Project for Public Spaces, are being started to create this "third place" in communities. They are taking form in independent bookstores, coffeehouses, and local pubs, and through new and innovative means to create the social capital needed to foster the sense and spirit of community. Pope John Paul II observed that "a community needs a soul if it is to become a true home for human beings. You, the people must give it this soul."

Western cultures are thought to be losing the spirit of community that once was found in institutions, including churches and community centers.

What is the *soul* of your community? How safe do people feel? Do they feel that they belong?

HOW ADAPTABLE AND OPEN TO CHANGE IS YOUR COMMUNITY?

Over the years, I have had the opportunity to consult with the Federal Reserve Bank, the central banking system of the United States. I am particularly interested in the work they undertake through the Community Re-investment Act. The CRA is a federal law designed to encourage commercial banks and savings associations to meet the needs of borrowers in all segments of their communities, including low- and moderate-income neighborhoods.

Congress passed the act in 1977 to reduce discriminatory credit practices against low income neighborhoods, a practice known as red-lining. The act requires the appropriate federal financial supervisory agencies to encourage regulated financial institutions to meet the credit needs of local communities in which they are chartered, consistent with safe and sound operation. To enforce the statute, federal regulatory agencies examine banking institutions for CRA compliance and take this information into consideration when approving applications for new bank branches or for mergers or acquisitions. Some politicians, economists, and other commentators have charged that the CRA contributed in part to the 2008 financial crisis by encouraging banks to make unsafe loans.

I was particularly struck by the number of barren communities in places like West Virginia, where there was no formal or informal leadership. Essentially, there was no hope. These communities were held hostage by extreme poverty. Other communities may be held hostage by gangs and other forms of social anomie. Witness the control that gangs hold over segments of the southern French city, Marseilles. Such total breakdowns in social order make the problems I experienced in Northern Ireland seem mild. The gangs in Marseilles have developed a whole new social order, including salaries for their members.

> As with personal health, the health of a community is hard to reclaim once the cancer has taken hold.

What interferes with the ability of communities to adapt and find solutions to such cancers? As with personal health, the health of a community is hard to reclaim once the cancer has taken hold.

DOES YOUR COMMUNITY EMBRACE DIVERSITY AND CREATIVITY?

While earlier definitions of community may have alluded to the notion of "sameness," today the progressive city is defined by its "pluralism." Often this pluralism is captured through the diversity of cuisine, fashion, and music. Assimilation is harder where language, religious tradition, or family practices are concerned.

To be sure, xenophobia (the intense or irrational dislike or fear of people from other countries or cultures) and racism still sabotage the richness of diversity that, when combined with creativity, permits the development of a community's "Third Circle."

My personal journey over the past forty years from Northern Ireland, via London, Indiana, Missouri, and now the New South, has been an interesting education in the fear and ignorance that perpetuates xenophobia and racism. But those communities around the world who truly have a "Third Circle" recognize that diversity is their ticket to the future in contrast to the stagnation that is killing too many communities that are stuck in the past—their "First Circle." For it is diversity, in all of its manifestations, that unleashes the creativity that, in turn, stimulates the innovation that causes prosperity. When there is prosperity in the nation, there is peace in the world.

> But those communities around the world who truly have a "Third Circle" recognize that diversity is their ticket to the future in contrast to the stagnation that is killing too many communities that are stuck in the past—their "First Circle."

DOES YOUR COMMUNITY DELIVER QUALITY SERVICES?

Are the services in your community predictable, reliable, and dependable? As the global economic crisis filters down to local communities, many of the services we took for granted are being curtailed or even eliminated. In the United States, this may be felt in reduced trash collection schedules, library closings, fewer bus schedules, and more. As noted earlier, it is often the less fortunate who are most impacted. In developing nations, it is particularly felt in unreliable electricity service, not to mention potable water. Such problems exacerbate other issues; for example, increased crime, interruption of education, and public safety.

IS YOUR COMMUNITY ATTRACTIVE AND GROWING?

In my earlier book[5], I included a chapter entitled "Knowing What Attracts Others to Follow You." Its thesis was that leaders are attractors who engender a sense of safeness that followers feel regarding where the leader plans to take the organization and how. As I travel around the United States and the world, every airport I land at is selling its community even before I exit the arrival concourse.

Clearly, a major initiative for a community's economic development is the recruitment of businesses and jobs. This is often done through the local chamber of commerce or by specifically chartered agencies that may even support a whole region. What is it that attracts others to your community? That attractiveness may depend on your community's accessibility by air and road, quality of its infrastructure, educational opportunities, arts and leisure, housing, and general quality of life.

Are you a magical quilt of cultures? How satisfied are the citizens in your community? Are you—like Detroit, Michigan, or Gary, Indiana—losing population? Where do you fall on the "best places to live" survey?

To be sure, we may not have much choice if our livelihoods require us to relocate with a particular company, in a particular industry, with a particular skill set that we committed to early in our careers.

In summary, can we trust our elected and non-elected leaders? Do we feel safe? Are we embracing change? Are we an innovative community? Can we depend on the quality and reliability of the services we pay for through our taxes? What is the quality of life we enjoy? Do we think of our communities as home?

As with each of the relationships I have discussed in this book, the *a priori* question is do you, in fact, have a "Third Circle"? In chapter 1, I posed the question whether nations have "Third Circles." If they did, they would not be in the conditions they are in or be at odds with other nations to the extent that so much of their gross national products are consumed on military defense.

Regardless of the scale of your community, is your "Third Circle" characterized by integrity, is it proportional, and is it beautiful?

A community with integrity will truly care about its citizens. That will manifest itself in the security of political elections; the fairness of the judicial system; the equity of the educational system; the access to health and other forms of care; the honesty and believability of elected officials; the professionalism of governmental staff; the undiscriminating deportment of public safety officials; and the freedom for families, churches, and other voluntary organizations to mediate the host of support activities that provide the true fabric of a community.

A community with proportionality will be well planned. It will use the various disciplines of engineering to create ease of mobility, appropriate interpersonal interaction, line of sight to the people and things that nurture us, and scalability that does not suffocate us.

A community with beauty will please the eye with aesthetic architecture, colorful foliage, symmetry and balance, elegance, and charm. It will be livable.

> A community with beauty will please the eye with aesthetic architecture, colorful foliage, symmetry and balance, elegance, and charm. It will be livable.

Can you see in your mind's eye a community with integrity, proportionality, and beauty? Does your community enjoy these characteristics? Do you believe it is possible? Are you part of a small group of thoughtful, committed citizens prepared to change your world?

CREATING A HEALTHY COMMUNITY

Have you sought and found how to serve? Albert Schweitzer's observation was directed to the individual, but it can equally be a message to corporations. How might we leverage the **Paradigm** to help our communities achieve the integrity, proportionality, and beauty of their "Third Circles"? How do we develop social capital?

HOW WELL DO YOU KNOW YOUR COMMUNITY AND ITS NEEDS?

The obvious first place to start to get to know your community and its needs is to subscribe to your local newspaper and community-oriented websites. To be sure, traditional newspapers have reduced in size, scope, and even frequency of publication; nonetheless, they are excellent sources of information and insight.

Local governments are constantly seeking representation on a wide variety of boards that provide oversight of community services. Most communities also operate public-service television coverage of council meetings, as well as interviews with public officials. Another excellent conduit to community service is through local universities and community colleges.

There are also a whole host of non-governmental organizations that carry the load for many of the services that care for the under-served. These include faith-related agencies, foundations, philanthropic organizations, and need-specific initiatives.

HOW DO YOU DEMONSTRATE RESPECT FOR YOUR COMMUNITY?

President Kennedy, during his 1961 inaugural address, challenged us to "ask not what your country can do for you—ask what you can do for your country." These words are particularly true at the local level, for so much of the quality of life we enjoy and our public safety depends upon the vigilance of citizens. This commitment to service starts early in childhood and reflects the quality of socialization.

Socialization is learning to adopt the behavior patterns of the community. It is how young people develop the skills and knowledge and learn the roles necessary to function within their cultures and social environments. Ideally, this is accomplished before the age of ten. But socialization also includes adults moving into significantly different environments, where they must learn new sets of behaviors. Personally, I recall the challenges when moving into new cultures both in Europe and the United States.

Some of the most dangerous examples of disrespect in a community are discrimination, racism, and xenophobia. As stated throughout this book, respect for diversity is a criterion for organizational and social success.

HOW WELL DO YOU LISTEN TO YOUR COMMUNITY'S NEEDS?

The late Scott Peck believed that true community is the "process of deep respect and true listening for the needs of the people in the community." This true listening will help you identify how best to use your time, treasure, and talents for the good of your community.

Community development is often formally conducted by non-governmental agencies, universities, or government agencies to advance the social well-being of local, regional, and sometimes, national communities. Less formal efforts seek to empower individuals and groups of people by providing them with the skills they need to effect change in their own communities. These skills often assist in building political power through the formation of large social groups working for a common agenda. Community development practitioners must understand both how to work with individuals and how to affect communities' positions within the context of larger social institutions.

> This true listening will help you identify how best to use your time, treasure, and talents for the good of your community.

The University of Chicago and the John F. Kennedy School of Government at Harvard University are leaders in the field of community research and development. They have developed and make available numerous tools to measure community needs and to facilitate community development.

HOW DOES YOUR COMMUNITY
COMMUNICATE WITH ITS CITIZENS?

Communication is the currency through which we build community and social cohesion. Modern technology permits instant information sharing. As we have seen in recent stress points around the world, such technology as Facebook and Twitter can mobilize passions but may not be able to contain them.

Effective communication practices in group and organizational settings are critical to the formation and maintenance of communities. The way that ideas and values are communicated within communities are important to the induction of new members, the formulation of agendas, the selection of leaders, and many other activities. Organizational communication is the study of how people communicate within an organizational context and the influences and interactions within organizational structures. As citizens we depend on the flow of communication to establish our own identities within the structures and to learn to function in our communities.

> Communication is the currency through which we build community and social cohesion.

Withholding information or our style of communication can exclude members of a community and create social alienation instead of inclusion.

HOW DO CITIZENS RELATE TO EACH OTHER?

In the United States the Fourth of July and Thanksgiving Day are the two uniquely American holidays. Most other holidays are respectful of historical figures or may be religion-based. Thanksgiving is mainly a family-oriented occasion, while on the 4th we tend to go beyond the family to join with our fellow citizens in the celebration of our shared values. I often feel that the happiness needle trends upward on the Fourth. On the Fourth, we convene in community parks and on The Mall in Washington, DC, to enjoy music and fireworks together. On these occasions, it feels as if there is heightened social trust. Trust is essential if communities are to flourish.

For years sociologists have been studying social networks. For example, we are connected by interdependency through such relationships as friendship, kinship, financial exchange, dislike, sexual relationships, beliefs, knowledge, or prestige. More recently, online networks have had a major impact on how we find work, find mates, advance our education, find clients, serve customers, and protect ourselves from predators.

Despite all the social networking, isolation and loneliness are at unacceptable levels. The late Kurt Vonnegut, a writer and humanist, observed that the most daring thing young people can do with their lives "is to create stable communities in which the terrible disease of loneliness can be cured."

WHAT MIGHT SABOTAGE THE HEALTH OF YOUR COMMUNITY?

If we fail to master the relationships identified in this book, we put the "Third Circles" for our communities severely at risk.

For instance, too many young people will never enjoy "Third Circles" for their careers since so many will never graduate from high school. The drop-out rate is frightening. The literacy rate scary! Our national tolerance for this state of affairs almost suggests an attitude of anti-intellectualism. Not only does the failure of our educational system compromise innovation, personal happiness and quality of life; it also cripples local communities. Do we have a "Third Circle" for education?

> If we fail to master the relationships identified in this book, we put the "Third Circles" for our communities severely at risk.

As I noted in chapter 4, 50 percent of first-time marriages end in divorce, and 67 percent of second marriages fail. Invariably there are knock-on effects upon the myriad of relationships families generate. While some divorces are inevitable, there are opportunity costs and unrealized possibilities that are hard to calculate. How do we teach commitment?

The trusted and effective leadership I described in chapter 6 is particularly important for community development. Community leaders do not have the same positional power that corporate leaders enjoy. Credibility is vital. I remind the corporate leaders I coach, and on whom I administer our **Paradigm-based 360-Degree Assessment**, that if they were politicians, how voters experience them could result in a short-lived tenure in office.

Political polarization is probably the most lethal saboteur of a community's "Third Circle." When the lower portion of the **Paradigm** is violated, then the stability of a community is fragile. When people choose not to know one another, selfishly want their own way, stop listening, and shout the other person down, then we might as well lock ourselves behind *doors*. In truth, that is what so many of us are literally and figuratively now doing—closing instead of opening the *doors* to our futures.

When we live behind our metaphorical *doors*, we have gone in the opposite direction from the types of communities we promised our children!

Reflective Questions

- Who are the formal and informal leaders in your community?

- Have you ever thought of running for elected office? If so, what prevented you?

- What have been your happiest or most meaningful experiences in your community, and why were they so pleasing to you?

When you can look back at your life and see how you intentionally used your talents, surely then you will have much about which to be happy.

Epilogue: An Intentional Life

At the outset of this book I mentioned that my company deals with three critical issues that detract from executives' success and happiness. First is the widespread erosion of trust. Without trust, relationships cannot be sustained. The second is the insidious toll that stress is taking on our personal and professional lives. The third is the absence of "Third Circles" for our personal lives, our families, our businesses, and our communities. When we experience all three at the same time, it is an accident waiting to happen and surely portends poorly for the pursuit of happiness. Conversely, when each is positive and we are intentional, we ought to enjoy a fair degree of optimism.

Regarding trust, there are a few themes worth considering. For example, if you hope to be trusted you must be capable of making and sustaining a commitment. A commitment is the foundation for loyalty, faithfulness, and friendship. A couple of years ago my daughter, Moira, came into my office frustrated by an associate's demonstrated lack of appreciation for the importance of commitment when working as part of a team. As she processed her frustration, she recalled how her mother had taught her the importance of honoring a commitment, regardless of the pain and discomfort it might result in. That lesson was particularly poignant during her high school days when peer pressure was most intense. That learning has become a cornerstone of her leadership credibility.

Can you commit to your profession, your partner, your children, your associates, your customers, and your fellow citizens? Remember that your reputation—and in business that is often all you truly have—is a direct reflection upon your values and your capacity to commit. As James Womack, the renowned biologist, observed, "Commitment unlocks the *doors* of imagination, allows vision, and gives us the 'right stuff' to turn dreams into reality." Without commitment, there is little hope of reaching your "Third Circle."

> Would you want to be in a trapeze act with someone who could not be on time?

Regarding stress, I believe that so much of the angst we experience is self-generated and is the result of our inability to organize ourselves and manage our time. I was intrigued to learn that Gandhi was quite critical of people who were not punctual. This inability to be on time and, by extension, to be respectful of others with whom we have a relationship, is more serious than offenders realize. Would you want to be in a trapeze act with someone who could not be on time?

Notwithstanding cultural differences, others experience a lack of punctuality as disrespectful, insulting, and self-centered, and presume that the offender is undependable. If this is a problem area for you, take a time management course, set your clock ahead of the actual time, and explore the underlying anxieties that may be sabotaging your credibility as a partner or as a leader.

Stress management experts caution us to eat right, exercise regularly, think positively, and get enough sleep. Ironically, many outstanding leaders are known for how little sleep they need. Moreover, they seem to have more time available to them than others calculate. Careful observation reveals that they accomplish this through exquisite self-knowledge, self-discipline, emotional intelligence, and efficiencies on every strategy they employ to reach their "Third Circles." As Lucille Ball concluded, "If you want something done, ask a busy person to do it."

Remember, too, that discoveries come to prepared minds. When you have a "Third Circle," you know exactly the choice you should make, the *door* you should open, the *door* you should close, and the actions you should take.

Whether managing your career or your finances (both are huge stressors), keep your resume and your financial statement up to date. I had an interesting conversation recently with the person who manages our investments. She had attended a leadership seminar offered by my company and, when she *got* the **Third Circle** concept, she was visibly moved for she saw that, without knowing her clients' "Third Circles," it was impossible for her to appropriately advise them regarding their portfolios.

> When you have a "Third Circle," you know exactly the choice you should make, the door you should open, the door you should close, and the actions you should take.

Regarding the absence of a "Third Circle," allow yourself to dream. You will have to compromise soon enough. Remember that nothing happens until it is imagined. Complement your dreams with training in public-speaking, sales, and strategic planning. Find opportunities to practice these skills in relatively low-risk settings; for example, in your church, professional associations, social clubs, or community groups.

Finally, happy and successful people have a bias for action. They do not mope around, expect others to make them happy, blame others for their challenges, or sabotage themselves. They get appropriate help when they need it and are constantly reinventing themselves. They have peace of mind, are givers not takers, and invariably have a well-developed spiritual core.

They know that they have a destiny and that the first five relationships identified in this book were, in truth, preparation for the unique contribution they will give the community from which they derive physical and psychic safeness. Isn't it part of our natures to improve our communities for the benefit of subsequent generations?

When you can look back at your life and see how you intentionally used your talents, created a loving home, raised emotionally healthy children, ensured prosperity, and created hope, surely then you will have much about which to be happy.

> Finally, happy and successful people have a bias for action.

Hopefully, you will avoid the conclusion of Sidonie-Gabrielle Colette: "What a wonderful life I've had! I only wish I'd realized it sooner."

ENDNOTES

PROLOGUE: HAPPINESS IN OUR TIME

CHAPTER 1: THE THIRD CIRCLE

CHAPTER 2: THE SIX DOORS

1. Amy E. Unell with Barbara C. Unell, *Starting at the Finish Line: Coach Al Buehler's Timeless Wisdom* (New York: Penguin Group, 2012).

CHAPTER 3: THE MOST IMPORTANT CHOICE YOU'LL EVER MAKE

1. John O'Donohue, *Anam Cara: A Book of Celtic Wisdom* (New York: Harper Collins, 1997).
2. 2009 Employee Job Satisfaction, *Society for Human Resource Management*, 2009
3. A. P. Brief and H. M. Weiss, "Organizational Behavior: Affect in the Workplace," *Annual Review of Psychology*, 53, 279-307, p. 282, 2001.
4. J. R. Hackman and G. R. Oldham, "Motivation Through the Design of Work: Test of a Theory," *Organizational Behavior and Human Performance*, 16, 250-279, 1976.
5. John L. Holland, *Making Vocational Choices: A Theory of Vocational Personalities and Work Environments, Psychological Assessment Resources, Inc., 1997.*
6. Barry R. Schlenker, Beth A. Pontari and Andrew N. Christopher, "Excuses and Character: Personal and Social Implications of Excuses," *Personality and Social Psychology Review*, 2001.
7. Avshalom Caspi and Brent W. Roberts, "Personality Development Across the Life Course: The Argument for Change and Continuity," *Psychological Inquiry*, 2001.
8. A. Howard and D. W. Bray, *Managerial Lives in Transition* (New York: Guilford Press, 1988).

9. Georgia T. Chao, Patm Walz and Philip D. Gardner, "Formal and Informal Mentorship: A Comparison on Mentoring Functions and Contrast with Non-mentored Counterparts," *Personnel Psychology*, 1992.

CHAPTER 4: THEN, COMPANIONSHIP

CHAPTER 5: THE STORY IN THEIR EYES

1. Stanley I. Greenspan (with Beryl Lieff Benderly), *The Growth of the Mind: And the Endangered Origins of Intelligence* (New York: Perseus Books, 1997).

CHAPTER 6: BEING WORTHY OF TRUST

1. Roderick M. Kramer, "Rethinking Trust," *Harvard Business Review*, June, 2009, pp 69-77.

2. Kate Sweetman, "Norway's Boards: Two Years Later, What Difference Do Women Make?," the website of *Fast Company*, July 13, 2009, http://www.fastcompany.com/1308538/norway's-boards-two-years-later-what-difference-do-women-make.

3. Constantine Andriopoulos, "Determinants of Organisational Creativity: A Literature Review," *Management Decision*, 2001.

4. R. John Young, *The Five Essential Leadership Questions: Living with Passion, Leading Through Trust* (Charlotte, NC: Keane Publishing, 2008).

5. John O'Donohue, *Anam Cara: A Book of Celtic Wisdom* (New York: Harper Collins, 1997).

CHAPTER 7: HONORING THEIR LOYALTY

1. Peter Drucker, *Landmarks of Tomorrow: A Report on the "Post-Modern" World* (New York: Transaction Publishers, 1959).

2. Peter Senge, *The Fifth Discipline* (New York: Doubleday, 1990).

3. J. Pine and J. Gilmore, *The Experience Economy* (Boston: Harvard Business School Press, 1999).

ENDNOTES

4. Thomas O. Jones and W. Earl Sasser, Jr., "Why Satisfied Customers Defect," *Harvard Business Review*, 73: 6: 88-99, 1995.

5. American Customer Satisfaction Index (ACSI)

6. James Surowiecki, *The Wisdom of Crowds* (New York: Doubleday, 2004).

CHAPTER 8: STANDING UP

1. Gillian Tett, *Fool's Gold: How Unrestrained Greed Corrupted a Dream, Shattered Global Markets and Unleashed a Catastrophe* (New York: Little Brown, 2009).

2. Ferdinand Tönnies, *Community and Society* (Mineola, NY: Courier Dover Publications, 2011).

3. Robert D. Putnam, *Bowling Alone: The Collapse and Revival of American Community* (New York: Simon & Schuster, 2000).

4. Ray Oldenburg, *The Great Good Place* (Emeryville, CA: Marlowe & Company, 1991).

5. R. John Young, *The Five Essential Leadership Questions: Living with Passion, Leading Through Trust* (Charlotte, NC: Keane Publishing, 2008).

EPILOGUE: AN INTENTIONAL LIFE

ACKNOWLEDGEMENTS

I am particularly grateful to my friend Fintan Muldoon for his insights regarding the structure and content of this book as well as his patience and commitment to helping me make it a reality.

I am also appreciative of the thoughtful reviews by Don Borut, Kevin Denny, Steve Ellington, John Fayad, Kathryn Murphy, Philippe Petot, Craig Philip, and Mary Pat Young. In addition, my thanks go out to Finian Carney, Carolyn Coleman, Chris Conway, Mike Cornell, John Gant, Chris Hoene, Ernest Jenkins, Dave Kosuda, Greg Lashutka, Ron Pelt, Jim Poppell, Leslie Riggs, and Derek Steed who also read various iterations of the manuscript.

The assistance of Stacy Cassio, Emily Jenkins, Moira LoCascio, and Seán Young with so many of the technical issues surrounding the production of a book was a God-send.

Finally, I am, once again, indebted to my dear friend Jal Mistri for his editing assistance.